PRESENTED TO:

_____

FROM:

_____

DATE:

Devotions
for Leaders

Devotions
for Leaders

LIVING
YOUR FAITH
9-5 IN A
WORLD

HARRIET CROSBY

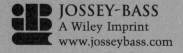

JOSSEY-BASS
A Wiley Imprint
www.josseybass.com

Published by Jossey-Bass
A Wiley Imprint
989 Market Street, San Francisco, CA 94103-1741
www.josseybass.com

Jossey-Bass books and products are available through most book-
stores. To contact Jossey-Bass directly call our Customer Care
Department within the U.S. at 800-956-7739, outside the U.S. at
317-572-3986 or fax 317-572-4002.

Jossey-Bass also publishes its books in a variety of electronic formats.
Some content that appears in print may not be available in electronic
books.

The scripture quotations contained herein are from the New Revised
Standard Version of the Bible, copyright 1989, by the Division of
Christian Education of the National Council of Churches of Christ
in the U.S.A. Used by permission. All rights reserved.

Library of Congress Cataloging-in-Publication Data

Crosby, Harriet.
Devotions for leaders: living your faith in a 9 to 5 world /
Harriet Crosby.—1st ed.
  p. cm.
Includes bibliographical references.
ISBN 0-7879-5940-5 (alk. paper)
  1. Leadership—Religious aspects—Christianity. I. Title.
BV4597.53.L43 C76 2002
242'.68—dc21   2002007587

Printed in the United States of America
FIRST EDITION
HB Printing   10 9 8 7 6 5 4 3 2 1

Introduction

Being a leader is always a challenge. Otherwise, there wouldn't be so many books, articles, and programs every year on how to lead, how to improve our character, how to lead from our hearts, our heads, our guts, or how to emulate the best qualities of the leaders in history. Yet there are so many different styles of leadership, so many conflicting demands and expectations among those who follow us. How does a leader who is also a Christian navigate these turbulent waters with grace, hope, and mercy?

Amidst all the often-conflicting messages we hear about leadership, our God calls us simply to be faithful—faithful to the gospel given to us in Jesus Christ. Although God's call to faithful leadership may be simple, it is not easy. For Christ's gospel invites us to love and forgive, to have mercy and trust, to live justly and humbly in every aspect of our lives—a very tall order indeed.

Devotions for Leaders looks at the Bible with a leader's eyes. It isn't a Bible study, but a devotional tool to help us find the inspiration we need to do the best we can as leaders. The book doesn't give answers; instead, it helps readers reflect prayerfully on who God is calling them to be as leaders. Using quotes from the best books about leadership, *Devotions for Leaders* can help us find in scripture the strength, hope, and motivation to apply our faith to the ways in which we lead. Used devotionally and meditatively, the book can also help us hear the Holy Spirit whispering to us in the depths of our own hearts, calling us to become better, more effective, more *faithful* leaders than we are today.

May you find the wisdom, power, and mercy in Christ to be the leader God is calling you to be.

The
Character
of a Leader

Leaders Aren't Born, They're Made

> Put these things into practice, devote yourself to them, so that all may see your progress. Pay close attention to yourself and to your teaching; continue in these things, for in doing this you will save both yourself and your hearers.
>
> —1 Timothy 4:15–16

Becoming a leader is a lot like investing successfully in the stock market. If your hope is to make a fortune in a day, you're not going to be successful. What matters most is the long haul. My friend Tag Short maintains, "The secret of our success is found in our daily agenda." If you continually invest in your leadership development, letting your "assets" compound, the inevitable result is growth over time.[1]

There's an old joke: a tourist stops a New Yorker in Manhattan and asks, "How do I get to Carnegie Hall?" "Practice, practice, practice" is the reply. How do we get to be effective, faithful leaders? The answer is the same: it takes practice every day of our lives. Very few leaders are born leaders; most of us have to work at our leadership skills diligently every day. And even those of us gifted at leadership from an early age know the power of practicing the art of leadership daily.

Becoming a leader is like growing in faith. Being a Christian is not only a conscious decision to follow Christ; it is a daily journey we make with our entire lives as we follow Jesus doggedly, step by step. Being a leader is a daily journey, too. It's what Paul was telling Timothy when he exhorted him to put what he learned into practice and to continue in them, for Timothy's sake and for the sake of the church Timothy led. Like faith, we devote ourselves to practicing daily what we have learned about leadership from God, our mentors and teachers, and our organizations. Success is found in our daily agendas—the decisions we make, the relationships we choose and cultivate, how we exercise and share our power. It's also about how we choose to spend our time, and the care we put into communicating with the people in our organizations and how well we listen to them—among many other things.

Skim through the last couple of months of your daily calendar or personal organizer. What does it tell you about how you are practicing your leadership skills? Is there something missing, some skill or capability you need to develop? If so, ask God to help you integrate whatever may be missing into your daily life as a leader and put these things into practice so that all may see your progress.

> *Help me, O Lord, to practice being a leader every day even as I seek to follow after you. Amen.*[2]
>
> —ROBERT QUINN

Integrity Is Good Business

> But be doers of the word, and not merely hearers who deceive themselves. For if any are hearers of the word and not doers, they are like those who look at themselves in a mirror; for they look at themselves and, on going away, immediately forget what they were like. But those who look into the perfect law, the law of liberty, and persevere, being not hearers who forget but doers who act—they will be blessed in their doing.
>
> —James 1:22–25

St. Benedict, being both very spiritual and a practical man, counsels the abbot to form and instruct the monastic community not only with words but also by his good behavior. In the Rule he prescribes, "Furthermore, anyone who receives the name of abbot is to lead his disciples by a two-fold teaching; he must point out to them all that is good and holy more by example than by words."[3]

The life of faith can be boiled down to this: that as God's people we live as we believe. Because God does what God says, we do what we say. There is no disconnect between our faith and our lives. This is integrity.

A few years ago I worked for a company that prided itself on its ecological consciousness. The company's products and how it conducted business were environmentally, even morally, superior, the company claimed, to the products and conduct of other companies. Company leaders constantly told employees how lucky they were to work for a company that held nature in such high regard. But there was a disconnect: it slowly leaked out that the executive management regularly used deceitful business practices with vendors and competitors. As management lies and cover-ups were exposed, the company's moral reputation with employees and customers was irrevocably damaged. Morale and sales plummeted. The company was sold a couple years later.

In leadership, integrity is everything. Our employees, members, customers, and constituents watch us carefully to see that we do what we say we believe. We lead people with integrity through example—it's that simple. The hard part is resisting the temptation to give in to the easy way, to take moral shortcuts to get some quick success. But the way of God's blessing, the way of good business, is paved with our integrity.

> *O God, help me to keep my words and my actions integrated and rooted in you. May people follow me because they see that I am a person of integrity, a person of faith.*
> *Amen.*

Learning from Conflict

The fear of the Lord is instruction in wisdom,
And humility goes before honor.

—PROVERBS 15:33

Out of this experience emerged our official Silent
Witness (a national initiative to eliminate domestic
violence-related murders by the year 2010) guide
to conflict. . . . It consists of five simple steps:

1. Listen, and take notes if necessary.
2. Treat everyone with respect.
3. Negotiate on the things you can reasonably
   change.
4. Know what your basic principles are, and never
   violate them.
5. Engage in no revenge or retaliation.[4]

Part of a leader's job is to manage conflict.
When managed well, conflict—the irritating
rub of two (or more) opposing forces—can
ultimately help our organizations learn and grow
and move into the future with renewed strength
and purpose. And it can make us wiser leaders.
But managing conflict is hard, often uncomfortable, work.

A leader in the company I work for believes that conflict is bad and that conformity—to her ideas—is best. When alternative views are presented to her, or when she is challenged directly, this leader's response is to raise her "deflector shields." She shuts out all ideas or courses of action that conflict with hers. The result is stagnation—for herself and the group she leads.

I've learned a lot by watching this leader. I've learned that managing conflict well requires that I remember Proverbs 15:33 and start from a position of humility. When my views or actions are challenged, I must remember that I don't have all the answers and that others may be able to make me a little wiser. I listen humbly, which allows me to hear people with respect. Humility frees me to negotiate, yet to articulate my basic principles without violating them. Holding fast to a humble spirit, I'm also freed from the compulsion to retaliate or engage in inappropriate behavior.

> *When conflict arises, O Lord, grant me a humble spirit, that I may learn and grow by rubbing up against others. Amen.*

Telling the Truth

> Let your word be "Yes, Yes," or "No, No"; anything more
> than this comes from the evil one.
>
> —MATTHEW 5:37

> We keep relearning the lesson that it all starts with
> credibility. In our continuing research on the quali-
> ties that people look for and admire in their lead-
> ers, time and again we find that, more than
> anything, people want leaders who are credible.
> Credibility is the foundation of leadership. Period.[5]

One of the dangers I've encountered working
in corporate communications over the years
is the temptation to "spin"—to put a positive spin
on any company story no matter how bad the
news. But spinning is how our company got to be
in such bad financial shape. The company's former
leadership "spun" the financial numbers to
employees and our owners and effectively hid poor
financial results from them for a long time. When
the bad numbers finally came to light, as lies and
half-truths always do, our owners installed a new
leadership team. And we in corporate communications helped them get the truth out to employees about the dire straits the company was in.

THE CHARACTER OF A LEADER

The power of truth is an amazing thing. Simple credibility is a powerful motivator. As bad as the news is about our company's financial results, employees thanked us for telling it like it is so that now they can get down to work and fix what's broken. And the credibility of our new leadership team is amazingly high. With that solid credibility to rely on, our new leaders can ask anything of employees—and employees are only too happy to roll up their sleeves and get down to the hard work of turning our company around.

I've learned that the best weapons against the temptation to spin are the words of Jesus: "Let your word be 'Yes, Yes,' or 'No, No.'" Spin comes from the evil one, who is interested only in our slavery. Only credibility, only the truth can set our organizations free.

> *O God, give me the strength, the courage and the wisdom to tell the truth as simply as I can. Amen.*

Freedom in Responsibility

So then, friends, we are children, not of the slave but of the free woman. For freedom Christ has set us free. Stand firm, therefore, and do not submit again to a yoke of slavery.

—GALATIANS 4:31–5:1

Foster the taking of responsibility. The organization and its people must be responsible for meeting the organization's overall mission. But if you try to govern *how* people accomplish the goal, you won't be able to hold them accountable for the results. Let them decide the how. Then measure the success together.[6]

There is real freedom in responsibility. The best people in our organizations sense this, and they revel in taking on more responsibility— so long as we, their leaders, give them the freedom to create the "how" that will achieve the results they are responsible for. Good people on our staff want to be held accountable, they want to participate in success. The quickest way to kill motivation and excitement in good, responsible people is to always tell them what to do and how to do it; it denies them participation in success. The best leaders attract the best staff by giving their people a goal and letting them figure out how to accomplish that goal—afterwards measuring success together.

There is real freedom in responsibility for leaders, too. One of the most ancient spiritual practices is the discipline of "letting go, and letting God." The practice of letting go is possible because we experience freedom in Christ. We are free to let go and let God work in our organizations—because we can trust God, the author of our freedom. We do not treat our people as paid slaves. We resist the temptation to micromanage, to be overly directive, or to do their work for them. Our responsibility as Christian leaders is to give our best people the freedom to work responsibly and then hold them accountable for the results. We let go and let God work through our people. We stand firm, therefore, and do not submit—or let our people submit—again to a yoke of slavery.

> *Help me to let go, O God, and watch you work through my staff today. Amen.*

Too Much of a Good Thing

Do not be conformed to this world, but be transformed by the renewing of your minds, so that you may discern what is the will of God—what is good and acceptable and perfect.

—ROMANS 12:2

I realized that people wanted for themselves not something that was missing in them—and that others might think important for them to have—but more of what was already their special attribute. . . . The difficulty for all of us is that our absorption with what we do well may blind us to what will enable us to do even better. The particular challenge for managers is to remain mindful that organizations can set themselves up for trouble when they rely solely on the things they are already doing well and fail to see what they *really* need to do.[7]

Writer Lillian Hellman once said, "It is a mark of many famous people that they cannot part with their brightest hour: what worked once must always work." While I am not a famous person, I learned the falsity of relying too much on the notion that what worked once must always work. I relied too heavily on my special attribute as an articulate communicator while I tried to serve as a minister in a local church. I learned that reasonably intelligent preaching, teaching, writing, and discourse alone did not ensure my success as a pastor. I learned that what most churches want in a minister is someone who cares and shows God's love by simply being there and *listening*—not talking. I was blinded by what I had done very well and been rewarded for for years outside the church. Then, when the context changed and I became a minister, what had worked once for me as a leader no longer worked at all. And I left the ministry because I failed to see what God *really* needed me to do.

God wants leaders who are willing to be transformed by the renewing of their minds so that they can better understand God's will. As long as we cling to those attitudes and behaviors that made us successful in the past, our ability to discern what God is doing now, or what God is calling us to do in the future, will be clouded. It's guaranteed that our context for leadership—our organizations and markets—will change. To continue to lead effectively requires that our minds expand and that our spirits transform, so that we can honor God's call in those new contexts. The hard work of transformation is being willing to want what we *really* need to serve God as leaders.

> *Keep my mind and spirit supple, O God,*
> *that I may be transformed into the leader*
> *you need me to be. Amen.*

Just Do It

In toil there is profit,
but mere talk leads only
to poverty.
—Proverbs 14:23

The notion that people need to communicate
more is perhaps the most widely accepted idea in
management—indeed, in all human relationships.
Whether it's called "counseling," "team building,"
"conflict resolution," or "negotiating," it all boils
down to one idea—that if we talk it over, things
will get better.

Well, yes and no. I certainly won't say that we don't
need to talk. But communication, like everything
else in human affairs, seldom works the way we
think it does. Most organizations, in fact, are overcommunicating: meetings, conferences, memos,
phone calls, and electronic mail overwhelm managers and employees alike. Increasingly, we seem to
believe that everybody should be in on everything.[8]

I am a professional communicator. I have years of
experience in corporate and marketing communications at many different companies and in a
variety of industries. I am absolutely convinced of

the power of effective communication in building successful organizations. But I am also convinced that communication—no matter how good—is no substitute for good, old-fashioned *action*.

The company I work for is in love with consensus. We spend lots of time and money on teams and meetings and communications designed to build consensus among the stakeholders of almost any issue. One of our company's deeply held values is that "everybody should be in on everything." Even now, with our company tottering on the brink of financial ruin, we can't wean ourselves from overcommunicating in order to build consensus. Now, more than ever, we've got to just do something—sell something, boost revenue, reduce expenses—anything, everything. But we continue to confuse endless discussion and consensus building with action. We need to stop talking and get to work.

This experience has shown me the power of asking for forgiveness rather than permission. Swift, decisive action is a responsibility of leadership. Constant talk leads only to poverty. Change is continuous within and without our organizations; it's far better to take action and correct mistakes as we go than to try to make a perfect decision prior to execution. The world, our customers and constituents, won't wait for us to get our ducks perfectly aligned in a row before we take action. Communicate, by all means. But we do it on the fly, trusting that we do nothing alone, that God is with us, supplying us with the love, mercy, and forgiveness we need to just get on with it.

> *Today I will act decisively, O Lord, trusting in your love, mercy and forgiveness. Amen.*

What Doesn't Kill Us
Will Make Us Stronger

> While he was still speaking, some people came from the leader's house to say, "Your daughter is dead. Why trouble the teacher any further?" But overhearing what they said, Jesus said to the leader of the synagogue, "Do not fear, only believe."

—MARK 5:35–36

It is hard to imagine how surviving calamities could be good for organizations. Yet we know that people grow and prosper not just because of the good things that happen to them but perhaps even more because of the bad things—the disasters, the crises. Such experiences often cause people to make major reassessments of their lives and to change them in ways that reflect a deeper understanding of their own capabilities, values, and goals. Organizations tend to react similarly to major adversity. It's never easy, but people do seem to change as a result of surviving calamities.

Calamities are an embarrassment to management and are not likely to be regarded as the key to success. . . . In any case, the absurdity remains: In management, we have no alternative but to try to avoid the very things that could be most beneficial.[9]

THE CHARACTER OF A LEADER

Facing nonexistence is a calamity for any organization. There is a very real possibility that my company may no longer exist in the next few months. As I walk the company halls and talk to lots of employees throughout the organization, I find that most people are ready and willing to make hard changes to save the company, even if it comes at great personal cost. The threat of nonexistence has had a very clarifying, focusing effect on many employees; most want to do whatever it takes to save the company from oblivion.

The problem is one of leadership. Our leaders are embarrassed by our present calamity; rather than speak honestly and courageously about what needs to be done, they have chosen a course of secrecy and silence. An operating council of sixteen key executive leaders holes up monthly in meetings that increasingly resemble a "star chamber"—and they refuse to communicate any hard information or decisions to employees about how they can work together to lead the company back from the brink. Leaders have decided to avoid making and communicating decisions that could be most beneficial to the company during this very real calamity.

And Jesus says to leaders faced with death, "Do not fear, only believe." Jesus tackles calamity head on—with no pussyfooting, no embarrassment, no secrecy or silence—only raw faith that can overcome oblivion. Fear only helps the forces of evil do their work in our organizations. But calamity, when met with belief, faith, and trust, can make our organizations stronger.

> *Help me in my unbelief, O Lord, that I may face calamity with courage. Amen.*

It Takes Guts

> See, I am sending you out like sheep into the midst of
> wolves; so be wise as serpents and innocent as doves.
> Beware of them, for they will hand you over to councils
> and flog you in their synagogues; and you will be dragged
> before governors and kings because of me, as a testimony
> to them and the Gentiles. When they hand you over, do
> not worry about how you are to speak or what you are to
> say; for what you are to say will be given to you at that
> time; for it is not you who speak, but the Spirit of your
> Father speaking through you.
>
> —MATTHEW 10:16–20

Much of the job of executive development is an
unlearning process—getting rid of barriers to perception and wisdom and judgment. Leaders need
to regain trust in gut reactions. To do that, we can
think of ourselves as sensitive instruments, measuring situations and registering visceral reactions that
are usually ignored but should be paid attention to.
It's not unlike dipping litmus paper into a solution
to get a reaction.[10]

Hey, it's a dog-eat-dog world. The marketplace is a jungle. These days, the organization that falls behind ends up being another
organization's lunch. And it isn't much prettier

internally. Our employees and customers have huge expectations of us. And when we fail to deliver on those expectations, their reactions can be brutal. How do we navigate personally and professionally through such a world? Well, it takes guts.

Jesus fed his leadership team to the wolves. The world into which Jesus sent his leaders was pretty barbaric. Jesus prepped his team for what they would experience—trials before civil and religious authorities, flogging, (Jesus tacitly hints at death)—experiences that would mirror what was in store for Jesus himself. And what were these leaders to rely on when the heat turned up? God speaking to them in their guts; God speaking through their guts to the world.

We navigate our own barbaric world by trusting our gut, where wisdom and judgment—and the voice of God—reside. And we speak and act according to what we find there, what we hear there. For our God goes with us into the jungle to meet the wolves. All we have to do is pay attention—and trust.

> *Help me, O God, to measure situations and register visceral reactions that I usually ignore but should pay attention to—for it is your voice I long to hear. Amen.*

THE CHARACTER OF A LEADER

Entitlement:
A Leader's Downfall

It happened, late one afternoon, when David rose from his couch and was walking about on the roof of the king's house, that he saw from the roof a woman bathing; the woman was very beautiful. David sent someone to inquire about the woman. It was reported, "This is Bathsheba daughter or Eliam the wife of Uriah the Hittite." So David sent messengers to get her, and she came to him and he lay with her.

—2 SAMUEL 11:2–4A

A leader is a person who has an unusual degree of power to create the conditions under which other people must live. . . . A leader must take special responsibility for what's going on inside his or her own self, inside his or her consciousness, lest the act of leadership create more harm than good. . . . The problem is that people rise to leadership in our society by a tendency toward extroversion, which too often means ignoring what is going on inside themselves. Leaders rise to power by operating very competently and effectively in the external world, sometimes at the cost of internal awareness.[11]

A sense of *entitlement* can endanger our leadership and threaten us spiritually. King David suffered occasionally from an overweening sense of entitlement, which may have sounded a little like this: "I can do anything because I am king. Because I lead a great nation, I am special. Therefore, I need not reflect or think before I act—I can take what I want. Because I am special, I am above any consequences for my actions." King David's feeling of entitlement was nearly his doom as a leader—and it definitely harmed his relationship with God.

There are perks to being a leader. We may be well compensated with generous salaries, bonuses and options; or we may have access to the executive dining room; or we may fly first-class for business travel; or we may work in corner offices with lovely views. We enjoy a significant amount of power that determines how other people will live. At the company where I work, executives also enjoy limousine service. All of these perks might make us think we are special human beings with different accountabilities. We may be occasionally tempted to think we *deserve* this treatment, that we are *entitled* to it, because of our inherent special-ness—instead of seeing leadership perks as gifts or rewards for doing a good job. Like David, when we believe we are above it all, we stop thinking, endangering our ability to lead and our relation-ship with God through our thoughtlessness.

The best defense against feeling entitled—and acting on it—is to foster a constant inner aware-ness of who we are under the eye of God. Like other people, we are God's beloved children. Like other people, we are accountable to God for our behavior, behavior that reflects God's glory. Like other people, we are God's creatures, who are grateful for this life. Like other people, we enjoy our work because it is a *gift* of God, not a divine right.

> *O Lord, defend me from entitlement, and keep me ever mindful of you. Amen.*

Leaders Have
Leaders as Followers

> We [apostles] are fools for the sake of Christ, but you are
> wise in Christ. We are weak, but you are strong. You are
> held in honor, but we in disrepute.
>
> —1 Corinthians 4:10

> Most leadership today is an attempt to accomplish
> purposes through (or in spite of) large, intricately
> organized systems. There is no possibility that cen-
> tralized authority can call all the shots in such sys-
> tems. Individuals in all segments and at all levels
> must be prepared to exercise leaderlike initiative
> and responsibility, using their local knowledge to
> solve problems at their level. *Vitality at middle and
> lower levels of leadership can produce greater vitality in
> the higher levels of leadership.*[12]

Recently, I heard an executive in our company
make the following absurd declaration to
explain why the company is in such terrible financial shape: "It used to be that we had great
employees and poor leaders," he said, speaking of
the time in the company before he was an executive. "Now we have poor employees and great
leaders." This executive suffered from a couple of
questionable assumptions—that leaders reside only

at the top, and that leadership has no responsibility for the quality of its followers. The truth is that followers reflect the quality of their leaders. And effective leadership needs to exist throughout the organization in order to succeed. In general, a poorly performing company indicates poor leadership.

In contrast, the Apostle Paul was a leader obsessed with the quality of his followers. He knew that his apostleship, his leadership, was in vain if the churches did not lead locally. Paul saw correctly that the churches—and each of their members—had to lead locally so that the world would follow. Paul was a leader who would do anything to strengthen leadership at the local level; he would become a fool, a weakling, a disreputable lout, if that was what it took to get the churches to set an example for the world. Paul poured himself out so that other Christians could take the point in leading for the gospel's sake. And when Paul's efforts worked, as they clearly did in Philippi, his strength as a leader was renewed, and he was filled with joy.

There's no such thing as poor followers and great leaders. Ultimately, we will be evaluated on how well our employees execute throughout our organizations. For our organizations to be successful in an increasingly complex, fast-moving world, our followers must take leaderlike initiative and responsibility around them. That means that for us to be effective leaders, we must work hard to develop leadership at all levels of our organizations. Like Paul, we are obsessed with the quality of our followers.

> *Lord, help my employees and staff to lead locally. Give them initiative, responsibility and the drive to succeed. Amen.*

Honor Among Leaders— and Followers

> Let love be genuine; hate what is evil, hold fast to what is good; love one another with mutual affection; outdo one another in showing honor.
>
> —Romans 12:9–10

> The more a leader is honored, respected, and genuinely regarded by others, the more legitimate power he will have with others. Depending on how leaders deal with others . . . , the honor followers extend to them will increase or decrease and the legitimate power in the relationship will increase or decrease. To be honorable is to have power.[13]

Our contemporary culture hardly ever mentions the word *honor* any more. The word has an old-fashioned, slightly military ring to it that just doesn't quite fit into our high-tech, high-change world. But not so long ago, people felt "honored" to be leaders. They took on the incredibly challenging role of leader for the "honor" of it. They knew that to be honorable is to have power.

To have honor is to have respect, admiration (even a kind of love), an investiture of power, and deep trust all bound up together in a big bundle.

A leader who is honored by her followers can require and receive great sacrifice from her followers; an honorable leader can move mountains.

What must we do to be honorable leaders? Paul said, "Let love be genuine; hate what is evil, hold fast to what is good; love one another with mutual affection; outdo one another in showing honor." Especially, "outdo one another in showing honor." Paul knew that honor begets honor, that the more we honor—respect, love, empower, and trust—those who work with us, who follow us, the more honor is conferred upon us. And if ever a leader knew that with honor one can work miracles, it was Paul.

Today, let us outdo one another in showing honor. Let us be honored to lead.

> *Make me an honorable leader, O God, that I may bring honor to you. Amen.*

Do Good—Always

Do they not err that plan evil?
Those who plan good find
loyalty and faithfulness.

—PROVERBS 14:22

The closest that I can come to it is to say that the leader-manager is a *moral agent*, a moral agent who is trying to do good for others. . . . Leaders and managers try to do the right thing in terms of their own values and in terms of the organizational needs they can perceive. Not only do *they* try; those around them hold them responsible for trying and expect them to try to do good.[14]

I remember when the old CEO of our company retired suddenly. Shortly afterward, it came out that he had manipulated our financial results to hide how badly we were doing from employees and our parent company. I remember how *betrayed* we all felt. The old CEO acted dishonestly, and his dishonesty put into jeopardy all of our jobs, the very survival of our company.

Our actions as leaders have moral consequences. We have the power to work for evil or for good in our organizations. It's as simple as that.

There are no gray areas; it is impossible to do just a little evil so that we can get a greater good. I'm sure that in the mind of our company's old CEO, manipulating the numbers would buy more time. Not only did it *not* work out that way, it also brought down the swift and lingering wrath of our parent company, and it's doubtful we'll ever win back their full support and trust.

When as leaders we do good, even though it may be very hard or even unpleasant, the consequences are good in the long run. Had our old CEO been honest with employees and our parent company, painful corrections and reorganizations would have been made—but ultimately the company would have gotten back on the financial track a lot sooner. And had our old CEO done the right thing and dealt honestly with us, he would have reaped loyalty and faithfulness in the long term—not only from employees, but from customers as well.

Our God is a good God, who asks only that we return the compliment and do good as well. When we plan good, we find loyalty and faithfulness inside and outside of our organizations—and with God.

> *I will do good today, O Lord, to bring you glory. Amen.*

THE CHARACTER OF A LEADER

No Excuses

To another [Jesus] said, "Follow me." But he said, "Lord, first let me go and bury my father." But Jesus said, "Let the dead bury their own dead; but as for you, go and proclaim the kingdom of God." Another said, "I will follow you, Lord; but let me first say farewell to those at my home." Jesus said to him, "No one who puts a hand to the plow and looks back is fit for the kingdom of God."

—LUKE 9:59–62

Most CEOs find cogent reasons for *not* leading change, to wit:

- They don't have *time*.
- The work is *hard*.
- It is *risky* if they do act.
- They could just as easily *coast out*.
- They are *alone* at the top.
- There may not be a clear *reward* at the end.
- They don't know *what* to do.
- They don't know what *not* to do.

There are plenty of reasons for not leading, and most executives consciously or unconsciously excuse themselves from action by embracing one or more of what are, precisely, that—*excuses*. In fact, what they lack is appropriate ambition. And that is why the names of most CEOs fade from the collective memory, almost on the day they retire. We remember only the leaders.[15]

At the end of the day, leadership is like faith—there are no excuses for not leading change in our organizations, just as there are no excuses for not pursuing God. Leadership is hard work, fraught with risk. It's easy to come up with a thousand and one good excuses (see some of them in the preceding list) for not leading our organizations through and into change. The giant risk in leadership is that *we may fail* after expending so much time and energy for no clear reward. Faith, too, is hard work, fraught with risk. Living a life of faith means that we live in such a way that we trust exclusively in God to sustain us, to redeem us, to defend us. There are a thousand and one good excuses (see some of them in the preceding list) for not living by faith alone. The giant risk in the life of faith, of course, is that *God may fail* when we need God most.

For Christian leaders, the message is clear: "No one who puts a hand to the plow and looks back is fit for the kingdom of God." That's not to say that God will withdraw grace or mercy or love—there is always—*always*—forgiveness with God. It simply means that we aren't "fit" to receive such invaluable gifts. Should we let the fear of change or the challenges of leadership cause us to give up, then we are less fit, less able to enjoy the gifts of

THE CHARACTER OF A LEADER

God's kingdom. And why would we want to excuse ourselves from the boundless joys of heaven?

> *I make no excuses, Lord. I will lead my*
> *organization as I pursue your kingdom.*
> *Amen.*

The Leader's
Vocation

Listening for God's Call

> Now there are varieties of gifts, but the same Spirit; and there are varieties of services, but the same Lord; and there are varieties of activities, but it is the same God who activates all of them in everyone. To each was given the manifestation of the Spirit for the common good.
>
> —1 CORINTHIANS 12:4–7

Our work life, when taken up in faith, becomes much more than our doing a job. When the work of leadership is taken into the life of faith, it becomes a vocation. Leaders seek to respond to the call of God through their particular responsibilities. Thus one leader may join with God in redemptive work; another, if she feels called to lead, and if she believes that her talents and capacities are gifts from God, will seek to fulfill the role of leadership in a way that is consistent with her own sense of God's expectations.[1]

How is God calling me through my work, my vocation as a leader? How do I respond to God's call? How we begin to answer these questions moves us closer to the heart of working out our faith in this world.

We begin to answer by *not* answering—but by practicing the ancient spiritual discipline of *listening*. We listen for God's call, not just with our ears, but with our total being. We watch, we feel, we use our intellect to understand God's call. God speaks to us through many channels. Our staff members, customers, and constituents are one kind of channel. We listen to them for clues, threads, patterns of God's speech. What is God telling us through them? Another channel is our families. Our families can see how our work affects us—positively and negatively. What is it God is saying about our work through our families? Still another channel is our hearts. God's Spirit is at work in our hearts, speaking in the softest of whispers. Listening to our hearts is often the most difficult; to hear God's Spirit requires quietness, stillness, a cessation of activity, and a great deal of patience in order to learn what *we* really want and what *God* wants us to do.

One thing we can be sure of while we wait and listen for God's call is that each of us has been given God's Spirit for the common good. That's guaranteed. Our work as leaders is dear to God. And the God who calls us will give us the wisdom and strength we need to answer that call.

> *God, I know you have given me your*
> *Spirit. Help me to listen for your call today.*
> *Amen.*

Keepers of the Gift

> For by grace you have been saved through faith, and
> this is not your own doing; it is the gift of God – not the
> result of works, so that no one may boast. For we are what
> he has made us, created in Christ Jesus for good works,
> which God prepared beforehand to be our way of life.—
>
> —EPHESIANS 2:8–10

> "Ownership" [is] a term used to describe not only
> the literal owners, but more importantly, the emo-
> tional investment of employees in their work.
> Ownership describes personal connections to the
> organization, the powerful emotions of belonging
> that inspire people to contribute.[2]

I once worked for a large bank that gave stock options to all of its employees—from vice chairman on down to part-time tellers. It was called the "Take Ownership!" program, and it worked. My colleagues and I for the first time felt, and behaved, like owners because we actually were. The program was a huge success in reviving the corporate culture of the bank—and in reviving the bank's stock price.

So I don't disagree with the preceding quote, about the importance of "ownership" to employees in their work or in making successful organizations. But I sometimes wonder what would happen if leaders and employees were stewards instead of owners? What if we saw ourselves as the caretakers of God's gift—our organizations? What if we understood that we were placed in our organizations not as the result of our own doing but because *God wants us here*? Being stewards instead of owners unleashes a different kind of power: our work together becomes a sacred calling.

It may not be appropriate for many of us leaders to communicate to our employees that we are now all stewards instead of owners, but it's interesting to think about this for ourselves who lead by faith; we can certainly view ourselves as leaders who are stewards. For one thing, seeing ourselves as stewards keeps us humble; when we see ourselves as stewards, we can keep our sticky fingers off the controls and let God be God. And for another thing, seeing ourselves as stewards can enrich our relationship with God, and our work itself becomes a holy act of grace, an elegant dance we perform in the arms of our Creator.

Today I will see myself as your steward, O God, answering your call to take care of your organization. Amen.

The Peacemakers

Blessed are the peacemakers, for they will be called children of God.

—MATTHEW 5:9

Sooner or later every leader must face the task of dealing with conflict. . . . We are beginning to see that beyond a certain point, adversary action, confrontation and nonnegotiable demands may be counterproductive. . . . That conflict should rage openly and damage the joint enterprise [would not be] the only bad outcome. It can go underground, remain unresolved, and do even more damage. Bringing unacknowledged conflicts to the surface is part of the leader's task. . . . Leaders experienced in resolving conflicts seek among the tangle of interests held by the adversaries those interests that constitute common ground and may be pursued to mutual advantage. They generate alternative possible solutions.[3]

Many leaders hate conflict. Conflict isn't nice. It makes everybody feel uncomfortable, sometimes even shameful; it can make us feel dirty, somehow. But conflict happens—especially in highly creative, innovative organizations. In fact, innovation and creativity thrive on a certain amount of healthy conflict. But too much conflict is destructive, and we leaders are paid to resolve conflict the best we can. We leaders are peacemakers.

Not for nothing does Jesus call peacemakers the blessed children of God, those who enjoy the most intimate relationship with God. It's hard, usually thankless, work to be a peacemaker. It means working and working with parties who are at each other's throats to find common ground, where the adversaries may pursue interests of mutual advantage. It means that we leaders, we peacemakers, must "generate alternative possible solutions." It takes lots of time, lots of talking, lots of searching for commonality. It also takes supreme effort to subsume our own egos, including our wants and needs for the warring parties, to pursue the process of peace. In other words, being a leader who is a peacemaker requires sacrifice.

But the reward is great, though invisible. As peacemakers, we enjoy God's blessing; we are God's children, held close to God's heart. God's blessing strengthens us to withstand and overcome the nastiness of conflict. It gives us the power to withstand denying conflict when it rages in our midst, above or below the surface. It gives us the wisdom to find a way for adversaries to work together again for the shared good of our organizations. Blessed are the peacemakers, for we shall be children of God.

> *By your blessing, O God, I will pursue peace in my organization. Amen.*

Qualities of
Excellent
Leaders

Confidence in Forgiveness

My little children, I am writing this to you so that you may not sin; but if any one does sin, we have an advocate with the Father, Jesus Christ the righteous; and he is the atoning sacrifice for our sins, and not for ours only but also for the sins of the whole world.

—1 JOHN 2:1–2

Leaders are vulnerable to the normal range of human frailties, from physical illness and moral lapses to eventual death. No matter how well leaders manage themselves, they cannot hope to lead flawlessly. In small and large ways, their shadows will fall over the organizations they lead. Faith can help leaders construct an integrated picture of themselves that includes their flaws and vulnerabilities as well as their sense of competence. What faith makes possible is not denial of or compensation for a leader's weaknesses but rather their inclusion in self-awareness. Faith in this context does not negate the leader's efforts at self-improvement, but it does allow the leader to accept his or her human limits without losing confidence in his or her capacity to lead.[1]

Leaders are not like Mary Poppins; we are *not* "practically perfect in every way." But too often our culture would have us believe that we are. If we weren't better or more perfect than the rest of our fellow creatures, so the popular myth goes, we wouldn't be leaders. It's a dangerous myth, because it sets us up for an inevitable fall when our weakness, our imperfections, our mistakes, or our sins, are one day revealed.

Our faith is the best antidote to the cultural myth of leadership as perfection. Our faith teaches us that we are *forgiven sinners.* Our faith teaches us that we are not perfect, that we are sinners, but this does not hobble us in our work as leaders. Our faith teaches us that we are *forgiven.* When those we lead inevitably discover that we are not perfect, we can continue to lead anyway because we are forgiven by the grace, mercy, and power of God's love. We can be confident in our ability to lead because we lead from grace into grace, sure that God's forgiving arms support us, redeem us, and give us the strength we need to lead for another day.

God, by your grace I am a forgiven sinner. Let me be confident today in the power of your forgiveness. Amen.

QUALITIES OF EXCELLENT LEADERS

Prudence: Vision's Partner

> See, I am sending you out like sheep into the midst of
> wolves; so be wise as serpents and innocent as doves.
>
> —MATTHEW 10:16

> Prudence is far more than caution, though caution
> is included. Though prudence consists, in part, of
> the ability to learn from mistakes, there is far more
> to it than that. Prudence represents a quality of
> wisdom that, after a long and intimate acquain-
> tance with the way the world works, can with some
> reliability predict what consequences follow what
> causes.[2]

Prudence is the tactical side of vision. In a
leader, prudence is a mixture of common sense
and some street smarts, blended with a hefty dose
of insight. Prudence allows us to size up a situation, determine a course of action, and foresee the
results and consequences of our action. A prudent
leader is a worldly-wise leader.

I recently read of a young tech entrepreneur
who resisted the temptation to take his software
company public during the high-tech IPO feeding
frenzy. He reasoned—prudently—that most high-
tech issues were overvalued, and he wanted his

company to turn a consistent, solid, old-fashioned profit rather than just promising future profit to investors. His prudence helped him foresee the bursting of the high-tech bubble. And while many firms around him have failed, his software company is thriving by turning in profitable results.

On the other hand, the absence of prudence can be potentially devastating. The new CEO at our company communicated successfully the urgency of our "turnaround" situation. He helped us correctly see that our company was on the verge of financial ruin. But, then, he imprudently didn't provide swift, decisive action for longer than three months. The sense of urgency among us evaporated rapidly, and complacency returned. Our CEO wasn't prudent enough to see how a speedy course of action could motivate employees, accelerate the turnaround, and perhaps enable him to realize his vision of bringing the company back to profitability.

Jesus sends us into our organizations to be wise as serpents, as well as gentle as doves. Our visions must be partnered with prudence if we are to lead wisely and effectively.

> *Lord, make me prudent today, that I may be a better servant to you and your people. Amen.*

Driven by Compassion

> When he saw the crowds, he had compassion for them, because they were harassed and helpless, like sheep without a shepherd. Then he said to his disciples, "The harvest is plentiful, but the laborers are few; therefore ask the Lord of the harvest to send out laborers into his harvest."
>
> —MATTHEW 9:36–38

As you take on the role of caring leader, people soon begin relating to you differently. They get the message that you're not out looking for ways to catch them screwing up but are instead looking for the opposite. In this environment, people open up. They no longer dread seeing you coming down the aisle.

If people know there's a caring leader in their midst, patrolling the organization in search of achievements to celebrate, it only stands to reason that they'll be stimulated to show you something you can honor and celebrate. The positive focus on behavior and performance . . . significantly improves morale as it moves the company toward higher levels of performance and increased productivity.[3]

When Jesus saw the crowds, he had compassion—*because they were leaderless*. Without a shepherd, a leader, the people were "harassed and helpless." The laborers Jesus spoke of are leaders sent out into the harvest by a compassionate Lord. In Jesus' mind, leadership is an expression of compassion.

The Greek word for compassion in Matthew 9:36 means a gut-wrenching kind of caring and passion for others. That's the kind of compassion that characterizes our leadership. The sight of our people—our employees, our customers, our constituents—calls from us a compassion that makes our gut turn with deep caring, and we respond by being the best leaders we can be.

As compassionate leaders, our leadership is an expression of our faith. To lead compassionately takes guts. We refuse to harangue and harass and we look for the best in people. We refuse to hide in our offices, and we move around our organizations, touching as many people as we can because compassion drives us. Our compassion drives us to take responsibility to remove obstacles and barriers to success for our people and keep our people from being harassed, so that they can succeed. Our compassion drives us to help. Our compassion drives us to lead.

> *Lord, help me to show my compassion through the ways I lead today. Amen.*

In Another's Shoes

Strive to enter through the narrow door; for many, I tell you, will try to enter and will not be able.

—LUKE 13:24

Central to putting others first is the capacity to walk in their shoes. Learning to understand and see things from another's perspective is absolutely critical to building trusting relations and to [achieving] career success.[4]

In the novel *To Kill a Mockingbird* by Harper Lee, Atticus Finch tells his daughter Scout, "If you can learn a simple trick, Scout, you'll get along a lot better with all kinds of folks. You never really understand a person until you consider things from his point of view . . . until you climb into his skin and walk around in it."

To put ourselves in another's place—to see things with their eyes, to feel their feelings, to think their thoughts, and to respond with understanding and compassion by doing the right thing by them—is one way of entering the narrow door. Jesus tells us that it's the entrance to the kingdom of heaven. Yet so few enter the door this way—by walking in another's shoes—because it's hard work. It takes time. It means choosing to understand instead of reacting. It means setting aside the comfort of my own agenda for a while in order to risk having my mind and heart changed by someone else's experience. It means allowing my course of action to be shaped by what someone else needs.

When I was in seminary I met another divinity student who excelled at walking in other people's shoes. Liz became a highly skilled—and successful—minister because she believed that the heart of the gospel was to walk around in another person's shoes, and she acted on what she learned. She knew that to enter through the narrow door of someone else's perspective was at the heart of ministry. So rare was this quality that people flocked to Liz to learn from her and to be led by her.

The goal of our leadership is to put our organizations—our people—first, so that they can succeed. As with Liz, our success as leaders depends on how well we can climb into other peoples' skin and let what we find there shape the way we lead.

Give me the courage, O God, to walk around in another's shoes. Amen.

The Gift of Good Judgment

Teach me good judgment and knowledge,
for I believe in your commandments.
—Psalm 119:66

I learned that in the White House there is one
enduring standard by which every assistant to the
president, every presidential adviser, every presidential consultant, must inevitably be measured. . . .
The ultimate and only gauge is whether you have
"good judgment." . . . Judgment is something that
springs from some little elf, who inhabits an area
between your belly and your brain, and who, from
time to time, tugs at your nerve edges, and says,
"No, not that way, the other way."[5]

In an attempt to regain profitability, the company I work for has reorganized. As a result, I
have a new boss. What I will miss greatly in my
old boss, Eve, is her sound judgment. Eve had
both feet planted firmly on the ground with her
ear always tuned to the ever-changing needs of the
business. Her decisions flowed out of a healthy,
active common sense formed by experience. Yet
she was flexible and agile enough to rethink prior
decisions and actions if she later learned that our

customers needed something different. I've never had a boss whose judgment I could trust more. When I needed to execute a decision Eve made, I trusted her judgment would always guide us to do the best thing for our company and customers.

Judgment isn't a quality leaders can learn; it's a gift God gives. Good judgment goes beyond the cumulative experience we've gained over the years, though experience is an important part of it. Good judgment goes beyond applying common sense, though a healthy dose of common sense is an important part of it, too. Good judgment is a mysterious blend of intuition, reflection, and decisiveness that lies in our gut, somewhere between our heads and our hearts. As leaders, we should daily pray with the Psalmist that God give us the gift of good judgment.

> *Give me the gift of good judgment today, O God, for I believe in your commandments. Amen.*

Saved by Foolishness

Do not deceive yourselves. If you think that you are wise
in this age, you should become fools so that you may
become wise. For the wisdom of this world is foolishness
with God.

—1 CORINTHIANS 3:18–19A

Most often what gets organizations into trouble are
faulty leadership styles, poor internal relationships,
and managerial blind spots. The delusional hope of
a troubled organization is that it will be saved without having to make changes in these highly personal areas. Perhaps the market will turn around, a
loan will come through, there will be a new technique to apply to handle a difficult employee, competitors will give up, or the new product will
succeed.

The hope is that no members of the organization
will have to make wrenching changes in the way
they work together, or in their personal beliefs
about themselves and the ways they make decisions.[6]

Leadership is a very personal experience. To
lead, we call upon a host of personal
strengths—a sense of humor, intelligence, courage,

intuition, faith, self-control, adaptability, values, and so forth—and project them out into the world for all to see. The flip side is just as public and just as personal. Though we prefer to think otherwise, all of our very personal weaknesses—stubbornness, insensitivity, fear, distrust, blind ambition, disbelief, and more—also affect our leadership abilities.

I work for a company that got into trouble largely because of "faulty leadership styles, poor internal relationships, and managerial blind spots." When market conditions changed dramatically, our leaders' weaknesses overcame their strengths—and they were unwilling to make those "wrenching personal changes" in their leadership styles and behaviors. Instead, our leaders clung to the hope that the market would change again in our favor—and they chose to do nothing but wait.

For each personal strength there is a personal weakness that can derail our leadership. God calls us to make those wrenching personal changes whenever our weaknesses threaten to undermine our service. We are to risk becoming fools for Christ's sake, so that we might grow in wisdom and judgment. We are to risk feeling like fools and take an honest look at our weaknesses and seek to change them in order to become better, more effective leaders—for God's sake. For the wisdom of this world—blindness and denial and defiance—is foolishness to God.

> *God, give me the courage to make any wrenching personal changes that will make me a better leader. Amen.*

Members Only

As it is, there are many members, yet one body. The eye
cannot say to the hand, "I have no need of you," nor
again the head to the feet, "I have no need of you." On
the contrary, the members of the body that seem to be
weaker are indispensable, and those members of the body
that we think less honorable we clothe with greater
honor, and our less respectable members are treated with
greater respect; whereas our more respectable members
do not need this.

—1 CORINTHIANS 12:21–24A

True leaders are defined by the groups they are
serving, and they understand the job as being inter-
dependent with the group. We have all seen leaders
who successfully move from one organization to
another even though they may not be expert in the
second organization's business. They are able to do
this because they define their task as evoking the
knowledge, skills and creativity of those who are
already with the organization. They are secure
enough in their own identities to be able to be
influenced by new information and to accept the
ideas of others in the group.[7]

There is a young executive at our company who is one of those true leaders—one who is defined by the group he serves. He has an amazing amount of product knowledge about the business he runs; and he is never afraid to roll up his sleeves and work side by side with his team to get products launched on time and in budget. When his expertise doesn't add value to a project, he gets out of his team's way so that they can do their jobs. He sees his job as leader as making sure the company gives his team all the resources, budget, and equipment they need to get the job done, and he rewards team members handsomely for producing exceptional results. Not surprisingly, this leader's team is one of the most productive, efficient teams in the company.

Our young executive would make a great pastor. He knows instinctively that we are all members of the same body, and he knows that rank and distinction among members can be deceiving. He knows that the best person for the job isn't necessarily the one who makes the most money or wears the best clothes or has a corner office. The best person for the job is one who provides a critical service that produces results for the organization. God calls leaders not to live by appearances, but by *service*. We are to serve our organizations; and we encourage and reward those on our team who best serve our organizations, regardless of where they fall on the org chart. To live otherwise is to cut off your nose to spite your face.

> *O Lord, give me the wisdom and humility I need to serve my team and reward those who best serve the organization. Amen.*

Leaders Know
How to Follow

Let no one despise your youth, but set the believers an
example in speech and conduct, in love, in faith, in purity.
Until I arrive, give attention to the public reading of
scriptures, to exhorting, to teaching. Do not neglect the
gift that is in you, which was given to you through
prophecy with the laying on of hands by the council of
elders.

—1 Timothy 4:12–14

The notion of being an Exemplary Follower is one
of the most challenging in organizational life, not
only because it is so difficult to master but [also]
because it is so hard to accept. In our leader-centric
world, reasonable people might ask: What is exemplary followership and why would anyone choose
to take that role when the social perks go to leaders? . . . The best followers know how to lead
themselves, and they've demonstrated personal
reliance that makes managers comfortable in delegating. Exemplary Followers take their responsibilities seriously, initiating and following through
with minimal supervision. They do not see themselves as underlings of the manager doing the delegating. . . . They see their work as different but

equal to the manager's in any given work situation because they know how critical the implementation role is to the overall success of the assignment.[8]

Effective leaders know how to be good followers. "Exemplary followership" is a great training ground for new leadership. Timothy was a good, effective church leader because he was an exemplary follower; he knew how to execute faithfully on Paul's direction. No wonder Paul refers to Timothy as his child. What leader wouldn't love such a faithful follower, one to whom he or she could delegate any task, trusting that whatever a follower was asked to do would be done right without any hassle? Paul never lost any sleep over whether Timothy was doing a good job ministering and preaching the gospel.

We are leaders because we are exemplary followers of those to whom we are accountable. Like Timothy, we execute with minimal supervision. We don't view our work as inferior to those in the hierarchy above us; we see our work as different from theirs but just as important to our organizations' success. Our superiors trust us implicitly to set the vision and direction of their organizations.

Exemplary followers are extremely valuable to our organizations. The Timothys under our leadership must be rewarded well—generously compensated and well praised, their leadership skills developed, their responsibilities kept challenging.

Exemplary followers are like gold—they make us (and we make our superiors) successful.

> *Make me an exemplary follower, O God,*
> *that I may be a better leader. Amen.*

Identify Yourself

Jesus went on with his disciples to the villages of Caesarea Philippi; and on the way he asked his disciples, "Who do people say that I am?"

—MARK 8:27

Servant-leadership is, first, about deep identity. . . . A senior participant [at the Bell System Advanced Management School] approached both Robert Greenleaf and Peter Drucker with a problem and asked, "What do I do?" Greenleaf immediately answered, "That comes later. First, what do you want to be?" . . . For [Greenleaf], servant-leadership begins with an enlargement of identity, followed by behaviors. The reverse order—enlarging behaviors to mask identity—is false, and people know it.[9]

When we were children, parents, relatives, teachers, and friends asked, "What do you want to be when you grow up?" We were taught from an early age that our identities are tied to the jobs or careers we choose. We learned that we "are" what we "do." Even now, when introduced to new people, we often identify ourselves by what we do for a living as well as give our names.

But servant-leadership, the kind of leadership Jesus modeled, begins with a deeper identity. It's about laying a foundation of "being" in order that we may "do" in order to serve our organizations. Our servant-leadership must flow out of *who we are*, a deep understanding of who and what we want to be. Jesus knew that his ministry depended on who people understood him to be. He knew his ministry depended on people not just accepting him as another prophet but accepting him as the Messiah, the Chosen of God. In the early church, one became a Christian by confessing, by correctly identifying Jesus with the statement "Jesus is Lord."

Our true identity, who we really are, directs, informs, and energizes our leadership—and our organizations. Simply "doing" the job of leadership robs us of the full strength and liveliness, the sense of mission and excitement, of leading—and it can dull the vitality of our organizations, too. But when we reflect on and understand profoundly *who we really are*—children of a loving God, touched deeply by grace and mercy, the apples of God's eye, held daily in the palm of God's hand—the ability to serve our organizations, to put their needs and wants above our own, comes almost naturally. Leadership that serves, leadership that flows from who we really are, is truly ministry, an answer to God's call on our lives.

> *I am your child first, last and always, O Lord, and all that I do today comes from who I am. Amen.*

Raw Energy

He gives power to the faint,
and strengthens the powerless.
Even youths will faint and
be weary,
and the young will fall exhausted;
but those who wait for the Lord
shall renew their strength,
they shall mount up with wings
like eagles,
they shall run and not be weary,
they shall walk and not faint.

—ISAIAH 40:29–31

If one asks people to list the attributes of leaders,
they are not likely to mention a high energy level
or physical durability. Yet these attributes are
essential. Top leaders have stamina and great
reserves of vitality. Even the leader of a neighbor-
hood organization is apt to stand far above the
average in sheer energy. . . Leaders may suffer from
a physical disability (e.g., Franklin D. Roosevelt's
poliomyelitis) or episodes of illness (e.g., Eisenhower's heart attack) but they cannot over any significant period of time lack vitality.[10]

A friend of mine recently married a CEO of a start-up company. This is his third start-up, and he's already planning the next one. His new wife refers to her husband as "the machine." He is forty-four years old, does not exercise or belong to a gym, and he's getting a little thick around the middle as he enjoys married life. But he has the energy of a sixteen-year-old kid. He rarely gets tired. Not only can this man can put in twelve-hour days at the office, he can also come home and continue to work or attend social events. He requires only a few hours' sleep per night. He is the most steady, even-tempered, low-key guy I've ever met. He just quietly and relentlessly plows ahead at whatever task is before him until it's finished.

I don't know the source of this leader's energy. God seems to have built him that way. Not all of us are as lucky as my friend's husband to have such stamina—but we do have access to a source of spiritual energy. For those of us who "wait for God," who put our faith in God, there is a kind of strength to go on that defies the limits of raw physical energy. As leaders, we may not always have the physical energy to sustain us, but we do have access to the power of God in God's unlimited mercy and astounding love. The secret of our strength is our God, to whom we open our hearts, our minds, our souls every waking moment of every day. And we mount up with wings like eagles, we run and are not weary, we walk and are not faint.

> *Let me know your strength today, O God, that I may not grow weary. Amen.*

Perseverance:
Never Give Up

> But those who look into the perfect law, the law of liberty,
> and persevere, being not hearers who forget but doers
> who act—they will be blessed in their doing.
>
> —JAMES 1:25

As one observer said of leaders, "They *never* give up." It is not possible to overstate the value of steadiness in leadership. Individuals and groups who wish to align themselves with a leader find it hard to do so if the leader shifts position erratically, whether from emotional instability, duplicity or flagging determination. Leaders symbolize many things, among [them] the capacity for the whole group to stay the course.[11]

If we truly believe that our judgment is sound, that our decisions are the best we can make, and that our vision is what's right for our organizations, then the best way we can serve our organizations is through *perseverance*. We simply *never* give up. Should the course we've set for our organizations need adjusting or recasting entirely, we act—faithfully, steadily, relentlessly.

The secret to perseverance is to always keep our eyes on the prize. The Letter of James calls the prize "the perfect law, the law of liberty," by which James means the gospel of Christ. Taking action on the gospel is everything; hearing alone is never enough. And James's letter preaches the power of never giving up, never ceasing to act on the freedom and grace we've been given in Christ.

With our eyes fixed on Christ's gospel, we do whatever it takes to lead our organizations well. It is our faith in Christ and Christ's gospel that gives us the steadiness we need to lead. It is "the law of liberty" by which we measure our actions, weigh our intentions, and set our courses for our organizations. And it is "the law of liberty" that gives us the freedom, the power, the strength to never give up.

> *The freedom of your gospel, O Lord, gives me the power to persevere and lead today. Amen.*

Principled People

You are the light of the world. A city built on a hill cannot
be hid. No one after lighting a lamp puts it under the
bushel basket, but on the lampstand, and it gives light to
all in the house. In the same way, let your light so shine
before others, so that they may see your good works and
give glory to your Father in heaven.

—MATTHEW 5:14–16

Principle-centered leaders are men and women
of character who . . . build . . . principles into the
center of their lives, into the center of their relationships with others, into the center of their
agreements and contracts, into their management
processes, and into their mission statements. The
challenge is to be a light, not a judge; to be a
model, not a critic.[12]

Leaders are principled people. We know the
principles we hold dear. Our principles are
what we stand on—principles that include honesty,
integrity, justice, and fairness. As leaders of faith,
there are other principles we add to the list,
including mercy, forgiveness, and even unconditional love. Our principles are not only ethical
realities, they are also very personal qualities that

tell the world who we really are, who we really belong to. It goes without saying that our principles are nonnegotiable within our organizations and among all with whom we do business.

As Stephen Covey says, "The challenge is to be a light, not a judge." Jesus thought so, too. It's easy to proclaim our principles, even to enforce them as would a judge. It's much more challenging to live our principles every moment of every day through "good works," so that all may give glory to God. As Christian leaders we are lamps through which shine the power of our principles—and the light of our good works illumines and leads all who work with us, who do business with us. We don't have to preach our principles endlessly to others; we have to live them. Every decision and every action we make as a leader is a beacon for others. Every decision and every action we make as leaders has the potential to give glory to our Father in heaven.

> *I am the light of my organization, Lord. May I shine steadily, clearly to give glory to you. Amen.*

The Forgiveness of Sins

Which is easier, to say to the paralytic, "Your sins are forgiven," or to say, "Stand up and take your mat and walk"?
But so that you may know that the Son of Man has
authority on earth to forgive sins—he said to the
paralytic—"I say to you stand up, take your mat and
go home."

—MARK 2:9–11

Many individuals and companies need to make a
quantum leap in performance, a healthy change
of habits, a major shift in patterns; otherwise, it's
business as usual—and that's simply not cutting it
anymore.[13]

Almost all of our organizations have collective
bad habits and destructive patterns we'd like
to see changed for the better. At the company
where I work, we suffer from a paralyzing condition of being unable to speak the truth to each
other. Collectively, leaders and employees are
deeply concerned with projecting an image of
being "nice people." The real truth about how we
work together and the company's condition might
produce some conflict, might upset some people,
might move us out of our comfort zone, and that

would never do. Our inability to speak the truth (and act on what we learn together) has deepened and prolonged our company's financial crisis.

I've often wondered what would happen in our company if we could all, up front, proactively forgive each other. I mean *really* forgive each other for the hard things we need to say, the hard things we need to do, to survive. But forgiveness is not easy. It is as difficult—and as rare—as healing a paralytic. The only way we can really and truly forgive is to experience forgiveness ourselves by the hand of God. We need to experience personal forgiveness from God in a very deep, private way in order to forgive those we work with. And even then it's terribly difficult. Forgiveness takes so much hard work, so much understanding and patience, so much letting go of ourselves and each other into the arms of God. As a leader, all I can do is try—to stay in touch with the power of God's forgiveness of me in the deepest recesses of my being, so that I can try, just try, to forgive as I have been forgiven.

> *O God, help me with the hard work of*
> *forgiving today. Amen.*

Blind Ambition

> But not so with you; rather the greatest among you must become like the youngest, and the leader like one who serves.
>
> —LUKE 22:26

Surely, the United States needs more and better leadership. And it is good for society, organizations, and individuals themselves when they step up and accept the responsibility to be *a* leader. But it is unhealthy in the extreme for all concerned when the individual's goal is simply to be *the* leader of something—or of anything. That's why you should start with a little self-assessment: "Do I want to be a leader to achieve a special goal, or am I just after the satisfaction of being in a leadership position?" . . . Remember, *appropriate* ambition is directed toward achieving the goals of an institution and realizing the needs of followers.[14]

There is a senior executive at our company who has transparently used his position to finagle an international executive position with our parent company. Every decision and action this "leader" took was calculated to get the next bigger, more prestigious job. His attitude is "It's all about me, and I'm outta here."

We've all known or worked for such irresponsible, ambitious organizational climbers who climb for the sake of climbing. Organizations across the country are filled with such self-proclaimed "leaders." The sad truth is that many people mistake blind ambition for leadership. But real leaders are people who want to achieve their organizations' goals. Real leaders choose to serve their organizations rather than rule them or use them to satisfy an insatiable ambition.

Christ didn't have a problem with *appropriate* ambition. It's just that those with appropriate ambition are the greatest among us, who become like the youngest, as the leader becomes like the one who serves. When responsible, appropriately ambitious leaders choose service over position, a little bit of God's kingdom comes to earth. When responsible, appropriately ambitious leaders choose service over position, Christ joins them—and all of heaven rejoices.

> *Give me the wisdom, the courage, and the power, O God, to choose service over position. Amen.*

Nobody's Perfect

Bless the Lord, O my soul,
and do not forget all his benefits—
who forgives all your iniquity,
who heals all your diseases,
who redeems your life from the Pit,
who crowns you with steadfast mercy,
who satisfies you with good as long as you live
so that your youth is renewed
like the eagle's.

—PSALM 103:3

Relax if you occasionally screw up 'cause nobody's perfect! And, more important, don't let the inevitable imperfections of potentially valuable role models get in the way of your learning from their experiences. It is self-defeating to say, "I can't use X as a model because X screwed [up] by doing Y." Instead, learners will ask, "Despite X's shortcomings, what can I learn from all the great stuff she did as a leader?" So learn from your own mistakes, learn from the mistakes (and positive experiences) of others, and remember what Eric Hoffer said: "It is the learners who inherit the future."[15]

QUALITIES OF EXCELLENT LEADERS

We didn't become leaders in order to be like Mary Poppins—"practically perfect in every way." We became leaders to serve. But that doesn't mean we'll do the job perfectly all the time. Like the rest of humanity, including other leaders who are our role models, we're bound to fail or screw up occasionally. When we do screw up, we've got to give ourselves and other leaders a break.

By the power of God, we can pick ourselves up and try again—and we can forgive the limitations of our role models. Our God forgives, heals, redeems, crowns, satisfies, and renews us. Our God removes our sins with mercy. Our God gives us the energy of youth so that we can begin again. It is not from our jobs as leaders but from our God that we receive our deepest satisfaction. And because God is the source of our strength and satisfaction, we can have mercy on other leaders who may have failed us. Like us, our role models aren't all bad; they're just human in the hands of an all-loving God.

> *I will not forget your benefits, O God, especially your forgiving mercy. Amen.*

Repeat After Me

The woman said to him, "I know that Messiah is coming" (who is called Christ). "When he comes, he will proclaim all things to us." Jesus said to her, "I am he, the one who is speaking to you."

—JOHN 4:25–26

Why is repetition of the Message one of the most important things leaders do? Because people forget; because people get distracted; because people get so caught up in the intricacies of their work that they lose sight of the purpose of what they are doing. . . . People in positions of authority believe—because they have imposing titles—[that] they can say something once (or twice) and safely assume that their people will have (a) heard, (b) understood, (c) believed the boss meant what she said, and then (d) committed themselves to act on it. Such would-be leaders don't understand human nature or the limits of their own power.[16]

Advertising professionals know the importance of *frequency*—how often an ad must be heard, viewed, or read before its message begins to sink into the minds and hearts of the target market.

Advertising people also know that only after the market has experienced the ad frequently does the market take any action, buy the product.

The messages we need to give our organizations—the visions or missions we need to share—are like good advertising. Our messages must be well crafted, simple, and repeated frequently before they sink into the hearts and minds of those in our organizations, so that they take action.

The writer of John's Gospel was a master at communicating the message of his gospel, the person of Christ. And he did it by repeating small words, such as *I am*. In John's Gospel, Jesus repeats himself as he gives the message about himself: "*I am* the light of the world." "*I am* the resurrection and the life." "Before Abraham was, *I am*." "*I am* the bread of life." "*I am* the good shepherd." "*I am* the gate." "*I am* in the Father." "*I am* the true vine." "*I am*." After a while, the reader of John's Gospel starts to sit up and pay attention; the reader begins to see the connection between Jesus and God; the reader must decide what she's going to do about this connection.

As leaders, we can do a lot worse than take a page out of John's Gospel. We need to repeat our short, simple messages until we're sick of hearing them. Because only then will those in our organizations finally begin to hear what we've been saying over and over and over. After a while, they'll start to sit up and pay attention, see the connection between our messages and their work, and decide what they are going to do about it.

> *I will repeat myself till I'm blue in the face, O God, so my organization will get the message. Amen.*

The Other Side
of Leadership

Be subject to one another out of reverence for Christ.

—EPHESIANS 5:21

Effective leaders of change need to be more than
just charismatic. Effective re-orientations [to
change] seem to be characterized by the presence
of another type of leadership behavior which
focuses not on the excitement of individuals and
changing their goals, needs or aspirations, but on
making sure that individuals in the senior team and
throughout the organization behave in ways
needed for change to occur. An important leadership role is to build competent teams, clarify
required behaviors, build in measurement, and
administer rewards and punishments so that individuals perceive that behavior consistent with the
change is central for them in achieving their own
goals.[17]

Leadership isn't just the sexy stuff, such as creating a vision, infusing the organization with
lots of charisma and energy, high-profile personal
exposure to large numbers of employees, customers, and constituents, or designing strategies.
A good portion of effective leadership also requires

good, plain old management and administration—
the hard work of executing an organization's vision
and strategies in a changing world. Sometimes,
great leadership and great management can be
found in one person. But with all the complex
organizations operating in today's fast-changing
marketplace, more often it takes additional people
to lead through management and administration.
For example, leadership at the company where I
work excels at making visions and plans. But the
visions and plans are rarely finished and executed,
because most of our leaders aren't effective managers, so not very much gets done very quickly.
We have been designing a customer-focus strategy
for six years and have yet to implement it. Our
company needs to add or develop leaders who are
good managers and who enjoy execution.

Management is an incredibly important com-
ponent of spiritual leadership. It's amazing how
much of Paul's letter to the Ephesians is about
management. He spends most of the letter directing how the Ephesian community should live
together as Christians. In fact, a casual look
through most of the epistles shows that the leaders of the early church frequently—and beauti-
fully—exhorted the gospel with one hand, and
with the other hand gave very specific management instructions on how to regulate community
and family life in order execute the gospel in the
world.

As leaders, we must concentrate on the high-level directions and strategies for our organizations, but we must also value and build sound, effective management. If we don't have the skills, desire, or time to manage and administer our organizations, we must develop, honor, and reward those skills among other leaders on our teams.

Lord, give me the management I need to help my organization succeed. Amen.

Leading
with Grace

Turning Jobs into Vocations

As he walked by the Sea of Galilee, he saw two brothers, Simon, who is called Peter, and Andrew his brother, casting a net into the sea—for they were fishermen. And he said to them, "Follow me, and I will make you fish for people." Immediately they left their nets and followed him.

—MATTHEW 4:18–20

Highly skilled, well-educated workers increasingly demand more autonomy in work, more satisfaction from work, and more meaningful engagement at work. Those leaders who understand and are sensitive to the need for meaning, and who value environments that help workers realize their potential, are likely to be more in tune with the new environment than are those who are insensitive to these trends.[1]

Having a job can be a grind, requiring enormous amounts of energy just to work your way through the day. Having a vocation can be exciting, the workday zips by because it's filled with meaning and purpose. Jesus transformed Simon's and Andrew's jobs into vocations—they became fishermen who could make a more meaningful, lasting contribution.

My boss may not be a Christian, but she imitates Jesus in turning my job into a vocation. She is always quick to point out how the tasks I do daily make a contribution to the company's goals. She enlarges my view of my work. By the time she's done with me, I see that I'm not just a drone in a large corporation, but that my work enables the company to be more successful. In other words, my boss helps me see that my work has meaning beyond routine tasks. And she rewards me based on the contribution I make to the company's results.

Successful leaders help employees discover the vocation in their jobs. It's not just typing, it's not just selling, it's not just fishing—it's using our skills to contribute to the greater good of our common life, and find meaning. If you can help us do that, we'll follow you anywhere.

> *God, give me the wisdom and skill to transform jobs into vocations. Amen.*

Learning from History

You shall tell your child on that day, "It is because of what the Lord did for me when I came out of Egypt." It shall serve for you as a sign on your hand and as a reminder on your forehead, so that the teaching of the Lord may be on your lips; for with a strong hand the Lord brought you out of Egypt.

—EXODUS 13:8–9

The best leaders we know all have this in common . . . : a profound respect for and fascination with history. This observation may be at least initially puzzling to those in contemporary society who agree with Henry Ford's view that history is bunk. . . . The leader who wants to understand what is happening in his or her organization can learn a great deal by observing and reflecting on the experiences of other leaders, even if they lived in distant lands and times.[2]

Our company has a leader whose specialty is corporate strategic planning. Before coming to work for us, she was a consultant to a variety of CEOs in Fortune 500 companies, helping them craft far-reaching strategic plans for their businesses. This leader is an avid reader of military history. She told me that she learned far more about strategic planning by reading about great military campaigns throughout history than she did in business school. She said that by reading history she's learned much from military leaders' mistakes, as well as their successes—lessons she can apply directly to her work as a strategic planner for our company.

Our faith is rooted in history. Our faith is the story of God acting in human history with love, grace, mercy, and redemption. Because we are Christian leaders, our faith helps us learn from our history—if we pay attention to it and listen to how God may be shaping us as leaders through the lives of those who have gone before us. Take Moses. Clumsy with words, even shy, he used Aaron as his spokesperson. Yet he was able to lead his people, not because he was articulate, but because of his intimacy with God. It was being the "friend of God" that fueled Moses' ability to lead a stubborn, thick-headed people out of slavery into freedom. By looking at the history of our faith, we learn that our ability to lead doesn't come solely from our own personal charisma; it comes from being intimate with God at work in our lives.

> *Help me to make the connections, O God, between the history of my faith and my work as a leader. Amen.*

Getting Feedback

Listen to advice and accept instruction,
That you may gain wisdom for the future.

—Proverbs 19:21

Unless we are willing to submit our sense of smell
to the criticism of those we trust will be truthful
even when they know their sense of smell is at odds
with ours, our leadership will be fraught with the
greatest of perils—the danger of taking ourselves
and our individual perception too seriously.[3]

One of our company's executives is a Christian—and he makes sure everybody knows
he's a Christian. You also need to know that our
company's headquarters is located in a suburban
office complex with a large duck pond behind it.
And the company just announced it would "outsource" several hundred jobs.

One of the employees targeted to be laid off
because of outsourcing circulated a fake memo by
e-mail that detailed how the ducks in the duck
pond will be outsourced. It was well written and
very funny—a bit of well-crafted gallows humor
that managed not to be bitter, harmful, or disrespectful to anyone. Eventually the e-mail landed

in the computer of the Christian executive. He flew into a rage and demanded that everyone who had circulated the "memo" apologize to everyone they sent it to. The executive didn't understand that gallows humor is natural in a downsizing situation. He was unable to listen to employee feedback that used humor to express some of the pain a large group of employees was feeling. He lacked the wisdom to at least "let it go." And his self-righteous overreaction only demonstrated to a great number of employees how rigid and unforgiving his Christian faith is.

We need to take ourselves lightly, gently, so that we can listen well. Listening carefully to feedback from those we lead, learning from it, and responding wisely to that feedback is a hallmark of Christian leadership. Our faith demands that we show wisdom, understanding, and gentleness to those we lead—because that is what God shows to us.

> *O Lord, let me listen to feedback. Help me to learn from it and respond wisely—and gently—to what I hear today. Amen.*

All Things to All People

For though I am free with respect to all, I have made myself a slave to all, so that I might win more of them. To the Jews I became a Jew, in order to win Jews. . . . To the weak I became weak, so that I might win the weak. I have become all things to all people, that I might by all means save some. I do it all for the sake of the gospel, so that I may share in its blessings.

—1 CORINTHIANS 9:19 AND 22–23

For the sake of the health and well-being of the common life of the group, the leader must possess a willingness to be accepted for what [he or she] is not (that is, to be accepted as a virtual reflection of the organization's values and assumptions) so as to lead the organization to change to become what it needs to be to meet the demands of the future. Frank Zappa once observed, for example, that a revolutionary may be more effective in a business suit than in blue jeans. And everyone knows that you can catch more flies with honey than vinegar, even if vinegar is what you do best.[4]

A leader's repertoire of skills must include a variety of personal styles. Our organizations are complex, made up of a great diversity of people with a wide variety of skills and experience. Sometimes we have to wear blue jeans, though we're more comfortable in business suits. We need to be able to offer honey when the situation demands it, though we'd rather pour out vinegar. Using a variety of personal styles in leadership isn't dissimulation or deception, it's a sincere attempt to accomplish the vision and goals that the organization as a whole values. "I do it all," says Paul, "for the sake of the gospel."

I knew a Presbyterian minister whose ministry was highly effective because he had learned the art of being all things to all people. When anyone talked with him privately, his whole focus, his whole being, was riveted on that individual. It was as though there was no one else in the world for him but the person sitting across from him. And the person sitting across from him could be a blue-collar worker, an intellectual, a housewife, a troubled teenager—it didn't matter, because for the gospel's sake, he became who he needed to be to show God's love to that individual.

For the common good of our organizations, we sometimes must be willing to be accepted for what we aren't—a slave, a Jew, a good ol' boy, a corporate tool. After all, effective leadership comes in many styles.

> *Show me who I need to be today, O God, to accomplish your purpose. Amen.*

The Power of Honesty

> We have spoken frankly to you Corinthians; our heart is wide open to you. There is no restriction in our affections, but only in yours. In return—I speak as to children—open wide your hearts also.
>
> —2 CORINTHIANS 6:11–13

> Feedback is a valuable commodity for any executive. It can offer insights into your behaviors and thoughts. It can let you know how you are doing in your everyday work and how you are affecting others. It can help you stay aware of how the changes you seek for yourself may appear either helpful or disruptive to other members of your family or organization. Feedback can also help you evaluate things in the face of a setback or opportunity. . . . Others can prod you, poke you, tell you the truth, and reveal their perceptions of you.[5]

The seductive, almost hidden dangers that always lurk near any leader are sycophants—"yes-men," who tell us only what we want to hear. As leaders, we all know people around us in our organizations who love to be close to us. Attracted by our power and authority, or the lure of promotion and security, sycophants give us lots of strokes; they bring us only good news and hide anything they think we may find unpleasant. Sycophants can be extremely likeable people who can make life very easy for us. And therein lies the danger: we like them, and we want to be liked and loved and told what a great job we're doing. It's only human nature, and we are very human.

The problem is, it isn't honest. Without honesty in feedback from people we can trust to be straight with us, we're in danger of losing touch with our employees, customers, and constituents; we're in danger of losing touch with ourselves. There may be a lot that is good and right about what we're doing, but we need to see the whole picture, even the parts that aren't so good, in order to grow as leaders and to learn and apply new skills. We need to lead—and we can't do that if we've only got half the information, half the truth, about what's really happening in and to our organizations.

Because we are people of faith, we have the courage God gives us to open wide our hearts, as St. Paul admonishes, and hear the honest truth, even when it isn't always pretty. We are a forgiven people. We have the power to look beyond the sycophants to others who can give us balanced, honest feedback—because we can accept that we are not perfect and try again with the help of God.

> *Open my heart, O God, to hear the truth*
> *about my leadership. Amen.*

Get a Plan, Get Connected

> For surely I know the plans I have for you, says the Lord, plans for your welfare and not for harm, to give you a future with hope. When you search for me, you will find me; if you seek me with all your heart, I will let you find me, says the Lord, and I will restore your fortunes and gather you from all the nations and all the places where I have driven you, says the Lord, and I will bring you back to the place from which I sent you into exile.
>
> —JEREMIAH 29:11–14

Our plans need to be good maps telling us not where to go but how to make connections. A good annual plan tells everyone in the group how to make connections so that we can move on with our work. Simple discussion together—of the future, of the context in which we serve, of our strengths and resources and weaknesses—can be measured. How well do we discuss who we are and who we intend to be? You know, applying a yardstick to something really can give you a wonderful new insight as to what counts.[6]

One of the things expected of us as leaders is to have a plan. Good plans are maps that help the people in our organizations make connections to each other and to our customers and constituents. Our plans show our strengths and weaknesses and where we've come from and where we're going.

Our new CEO crafted a plan that calls for the company to break down the "silos" between its various businesses. The plan calls for more collaboration among employees across business lines so that the company can present one face, instead of many, to our customers. The plan also calls for leaders to improve two-way communication with employees. It's all about making connections so that we can do business better, turn our company around, and get profitable again. We've got a long way to go because the silos have been up for so long and have done so much damage. But at least we've got a plan, and leaders and employees are working diligently to follow it.

Making a good plan that makes connections for our organizations takes a lot of thought, insight, and frank discussion. And following the plan takes a lot of hard work and dogged perseverance. Need some inspiration? Just think about God's plan. Jeremiah shows us that God has a plan for our welfare, not harm, and a future filled with hope. God's plan is all about making connections with God. God plans to connect with us, to deliver us again and again with mercy, grace, and love that knows no end.

> *May the plan I make for my organization,
> O Lord, connect your people that they may
> better work out your call. Amen.*

Leading with Attitude

In everything do to others as you would have them do to
you; for this is the law and the prophets.

—MATTHEW 7:12

Managers with positive expectations set a climate
that makes people feel more at ease. They offer
positive reinforcement, give others information,
give others opportunity for input and resources to
do their jobs, and are likely to lend them assistance
and give them better assignments. Those with neg-
ative expectations behave the opposite. Now, which
set of behaviors do you think are likely to produce
better results? The manager's attitude influences
his or her behavior toward others, and the behavior
influences the results.[7]

Isolated in a well-to-do suburb, our company's
office complex resembles a junior college cam-
pus more than a place of business. I think because
it is isolated from the hustle and "buzz" of a down-
town business district and cut off from any direct
experience of competition or threat, that over the
years the company's culture has developed the cult
of "nice." Everybody is very nice all the time in all
situations. Open conflict of any kind, even strong

disagreement, is bad form. Leaders and employees value being nice for nice's sake, regardless of results. The cult of nice is, I believe, a big contributing factor to how our company got into such bad financial shape. The absence of creative conflict and tension, the silence of positive, constructive opposition, kept us from making really tough decisions to keep us competitive.

"Being nice" is *not* what the authors Kouzes and Posner, or Jesus, mean in the quotes above. When leaders express positive expectations for their organizations, offering their people resources, information, and assistance to do their jobs well, organizations get better results. In our company, being positive and nice is divorced, strangely, from any expectation of success. But creating positive, can-do, expectations and high standards helps our organizations turn in positive results. Likewise, the "Golden Rule" sets positive expectations that get results. When Jesus tells us to treat others the way we want to be treated, the point isn't to help us be nice, the point is to show people the gospel and the love and mercy of God. The result is the kingdom of God.

> *Lord, deliver me from being merely nice,*
> *and help me to behave positively for my*
> *organization. Amen.*

Out and About in
Our Organizations

Then [Paul and Barnabas] passed through Pisidia and came to Pamphylia. When they had spoken the word in Perga, they went down to Attalia. From there they sailed back to Antioch, where they had been commended to the grace of God for the work that they had completed.

—ACTS 14:24–26

Leaders are out and about all the time. They're not in their offices much; the demands of the job keep them mobile. They're attending meetings, visiting customers, touring the plants or service centers, dropping in on the lab, making presentations at association gatherings, recruiting at local universities, holding roundtable discussions, speaking to analysts, or just dropping by employees' cubicles to say hello. It's the nature of leaders to wander; it goes with the territory. In fact, at its root the word lead comes [from] an Old English word that means "go, travel, guide." None of these wanderings should be purposeless. Leadership is not a stroll in the park; leaders are out there for a reason. One of the reasons, we maintain, is to show that they care.[8]

We are leaders who care. We care passionately about the visions for and success of our organizations. Therefore, we care deeply about those who work for us and with us to realize our visions and make our organizations succeed. It is impossible to care in the abstract. Instead, our caring has feet. We get out and walk about and talk to people and listen and see for ourselves what's going on, what's working, and what isn't. I was working at my company for nine months before I caught sight of our old CEO, a man who had given up and no longer cared about the organization he was supposed to lead. I've seen the new CEO almost every day since he got the job, wandering around the office complex—and because he cares he's beginning to discover what's right and what needs fixing at our company, as a result of his wanderings.

Wandering around is what Paul and Barnabas did as they preached the gospel and established and built churches throughout the Roman Empire. Their passion and their love for God and the gospel literally drove them out into the world to change the world.

If we want our organizations to change our world, we cannot sit passively and hope our world will come to us. Like Paul and Barnabas, we've got to hit the pavement. We've got to wear out a lot of shoe leather to show our organizations—and the world—just how much we care.

Let me walk with you, O God, around my organization. Amen.

Just Tell the Story

And as for the dead being raised, have you not read in the book of Moses, the story about the bush, how God said to him, "I am the God of Abraham, the God of Isaac, and the God of Jacob"?

—MARK 12:26

Stories are crucial to leading organizations into the future. . . . The climb to the top is arduous and steep, and we need encouragement to continue the ascent. Stories are essential means of conveying that we are making progress and that the actions people are taking are enabling us to get there. Stories put a human face on success.[9]

I work in the corporate communications department of our company. I help manage the company intranet, which is now dedicated to reporting on efforts to turn the company around to make it profitable again. We have a section on the intranet called "Success Stories." It's a section that catalogs stories about how employees are getting results and moving the company toward profitability. It is one of the most widely read sections on the intranet, because the success stories give people hope and encouragement, telling them that by working hard together, we can save our company.

But as successful as "Success Stories" is, it doesn't hold a candle to the power of our CEO telling success stories during company-wide meetings. When he tells success stories as part of his presentation, employees go nuts. They love it, because a leader is personally recognizing their efforts by telling them that they are valuable, that in them lies the future of our company, that we can turn the company around.

Write down your organization's success stories on your computer or in a notebook. Make a catalog of your organization's success stories—and tell these stories over and over to employees, customers, and constituents whenever you can. When Moses met God in the burning bush, somebody wrote down the beginning of one of the best success stories in history, and Jesus used that story to show his listeners that the God of Moses, Abraham, and Isaac can even raise the dead.

Help me to capture success stories, O Lord, and tell them often to my people. Amen.

Bearing the Pain,
Sharing the Pain

> He called the crowd with his disciples, and said to them,
> "If any want to become my followers, let them deny
> themselves and take up their cross and follow me."
>
> —MARK 8:34

> What is required to guide effective change is . . . a
> new philosophy of leadership that is always and at
> all times focused on enlisting the hearts and minds
> of followers through inclusion and participation.
> Such a philosophy must be rooted in the most fun-
> damental of moral principles: respect for people.[10]

As a leader, Jesus respected people. He "en-
listed the hearts and minds of [his] followers
through inclusion and participation." Jesus didn't
just tell people what to do, he involved his followers in the gospel with his use of parables and stories. He treated his followers like grown-ups,
respecting them enough to let them figure out
their relationship with God and make their own
choices. Finally, Jesus invited his followers to come
with him on a journey that included sacrifice; he
didn't force them to take up their cross or impose
the cross on them. Instead, he offered to include
them on his way to the cross.

LEADING WITH GRACE

What does this mean for us leaders? We all know that successful organizations are created with a fair amount of sacrifice from both leaders and followers. Successful organizations exact a cost from their members, usually a lot of long hours and hard work. Jesus shows us that as leaders we respect people, we don't ask our followers to go anywhere we're not willing to go ourselves. And even then, we don't force people to sacrifice; we refuse to make victims out of those who staff our organizations. Instead, we respect our followers; we offer to include people on our journey into sacrifice *so that we can all share in the victory*. As effective leaders, we don't sit in our offices and hand out orders. Out of simple respect, we get out there next to people and work hard and put in long hours, inviting them to come along and do the same so that we can all share in success. We let people choose to follow us.

Being a leader isn't fair. Effective, faithful leadership costs; there are sacrifices we must make. But we don't journey alone; we journey with our God who has gone before us, and with followers who choose to share our pain because we respect them and want them to share in the victory.

> *I am willing to sacrifice, O God. I pray that others are willing to join me, not just in the pain, but in the victory, too. Amen.*

Leaders Are Lovers

> If I speak in the tongues of mortals and of angels, but do not have love, I am a noisy gong or a clanging cymbal. And if I have prophetic powers, and understand all mysteries and all knowledge, and if I have all faith, so as to remove mountains, but do not have love, I am nothing. If I give away all my possessions, and if I hand over my body so that I may boast, but do not have love, I gain nothing.
>
> —1 CORINTHIANS 13:1–3

Great leaders recognize that the perpetual lot of institutions in modern, democratic societies is flux and spirited disagreement among those with conflicting values. Conflict, tension, and turmoil are the order of the day—today and tomorrow. Thus, great leaders recognize that there is no single truth, no final answer, and that the process of leadership is a never-ending struggle to balance the constant and never-abating demands of those with different objectives. . . . Poor leaders cannot tolerate this discomfiting posture, and they attempt to resolve the tension by either giving in to the demands of those who are most powerful, or by issuing a command that represents their own will.[11]

We can't assume that our customers, employees, and constituents share our values; nor can we think they *should* share our values. Our organizations are filled with people who are very different from us and will remain so. How do we lead if, as the preceding quote says, "the process of leadership is a never-ending struggle to balance the constant and never-abating demands of those with different objectives"?

We love. We love our organizations with unconditional love. Christians who hope to be great leaders love their customers, employees, and constituents as God does. We love them for who they are, no matter how different they are from us. The unconditional love we have for our organizations gives us the energy and strength we need to balance all those competing, conflicting values and agendas. Without unconditional love, our jobs as good, effective leaders are impossible. Without love, we are nothing.

So when the going gets really tough, and the tension and turmoil become unbearable, what do we do? We go to God with empty hearts, asking God to fill them with God's love, a love that is big enough, deep enough, and strong enough to embrace everyone in our organizations. And then we go out into our organizations, loving everyone we meet as best we can.

> *O God, make me an instrument of your love. Give me a heart that loves my organization unconditionally. Amen.*

Disappearing Boundaries

A crowd was sitting around him; and they said to him, "Your mother and your brothers and sisters are outside, asking for you." And he replied, "Who are my mother and my brothers?" And looking at those who sat around him, he said, "Here are my mother and my brothers! Whoever does the will of God is my brother and sister and mother."

—MARK 3:32–35

Yesterday's tightly integrated organization, which could be governed like an autonomous political entity, is today turning into a diverse constituency in which it is harder and harder to say who is inside the organization and who is outside. It is not just that today more and more organizations are getting their work done through joint ventures and formal alliances. It is that the relation a leader has to his or her followers is getting less and less like *governance* and more and more like *alliance* or *partnerships*.[12]

My father just bought a Nissan Quest minivan that has an engine built by Ford Motor Company. Hewlett-Packard, a company that traditionally makes computer hardware, is partnering with European telecommunications companies to

LEADING WITH GRACE

bring wireless, mobile Web appliances to customers on the move. I once worked for a large bank that viewed its employees as potential customers, persuading employees with significant portfolios at brokerage firms to move their assets to the bank's investment subsidiary.

To succeed, our organizations must function in a world of disappearing boundaries—a world that is increasingly global. The old criteria for determining who's "in" our companies and organizations and who's "outside" them no longer hold. Our competitors may be our biggest ally to get at a hard-to-reach market. What this means for leaders is that we can no longer think of our business, visions, and goals in "us-against-them" terms. Our thinking and values have to be expansive enough to include organizations that are competitors or leaders in industries different from ours in order to accomplish more for our customers and constituents.

For Christian leaders, this is nothing new. In Mark's Gospel, Jesus is fond of pointing out that who we think is outside the kingdom is really inside the kingdom, and who we think is inside the kingdom is really on the outside. The Christian faith knows no boundaries: all of God's children have access to grace, mercy, and love; whoever does God's will is mother, sister, and brother. Our expansive ability to love beyond boundaries can keep our thinking and planning nimble. Because of God's love, we can form alliances and partnerships to promote the common good of our organizations across industries and markets and among competitors.

> *O God, there are no boundaries in your world. Help me to move beyond any boundaries in my mind for the good of my organization. Amen.*

Be Great Enough
to Be Humble

> For all who exalt themselves will be humbled, and all who humble themselves will be exalted.
>
> —LUKE 14:11

> A humble man can do great things with an uncommon perfection because he is no longer concerned about incidentals, like his own interests and his own reputation, and therefore he no longer needs to waste his efforts in defending them.[13]

God wants us to be great leaders. God wants us and our organizations to succeed so that the world God has made will be a better place. The secret to being a great leader for God—regardless of whether our organizations have a spiritual or secular charter—is humility.

Great leaders are humble leaders. These leaders often have extremely large and powerful egos. But their egos, their sense of self, their sense of purpose and direction are so strong, they no longer need to seek approval from "yes men" or defend their reputations or interests. Because their egos are linked to doing God's will or a purpose higher and more powerful than their own egos, these leaders are humble. Humility doesn't mean walking around shuffling our feet and saying "Aw, shucks! Weren't nothing. I don't deserve any credit." No, humble leaders who do great things let their results and accomplishments do the talking for them. Against the odds, humble leaders who become great leaders work hard to further God's kingdom or to help their organizations achieve a great purpose. Their energy is put into the work, not into self-defense or self-aggrandizement through reputation building.

As Christian leaders, our egos are bound to doing God's will, and we are no longer concerned about incidentals, like our own interests and reputations; therefore, we no longer need to waste our efforts in defending them. When we humble ourselves—work hard to further God's will through our organizations and let our accomplishments speak for us—God will exalt us and make us great.

> *Keep me, O God, from engaging in useless posturing, and let my hard work for you speak for itself, so that I may become a great leader in your service. Amen.*

Know When to Go

Now the LORD said to Abram, "Go from your country
and your kindred and your father's house to the land that
I will show you."

—GENESIS 12:1

No one . . . has a call simply to a particular place, as
good as that may be. The call of God is to the Will
of God. Consequently, though every institution
mediates the call of God for us, every vocation
transcends any particular institution.[14]

A friend of mine, a Presbyterian minister, had a
plum job at a large, very successful church.
Her office even had a view of the Pacific Ocean.
She was the director of the adult education program and was a wonderful teacher and counselor;
the congregation loved her. One day, at the height
of her successful ministry, my friend told me that
she believed God was calling her to leave her present position. She told me she wasn't unhappy and
that she loved her job and the church. She didn't
know where she would go—only that she felt that
she had completed the job God had called her to
do in that particular church. Not long after that

conversation, my friend resigned and ultimately found another position as a minister.

Contrast my friend's experience with that of the last CEO of the company I work for. For the first two of the six years he was CEO, he was an engaged, active leader. During the remaining four years, he seemed to lose interest, but he stayed on, holed up in his office from nine to five every day, letting his senior managers run the company. Our financial results gradually deteriorated. He left only when our parent company fired him.

A leader needs to know when it's time to go— not only for his or her own sake, but for the sake of the organization as well. God knows what is best for us personally and for the organizations we lead. We serve not our career path, and ultimately not even our organizations, but God's will. Our hearts and our souls must listen hard when God whispers to us that it's time to leave. And, like Abram, we must always listen for God's call, be prepared to leave our comfortable situations, and follow God to the place that God will show us.

> *Lord, Let me hear you when you tell me it's time to go, and give me the courage to follow your will. Amen.*

Sacrifice:
Don't Go There Alone

Therefore, since we are surrounded by so great a cloud of witnesses, let us also lay aside every weight and the sin that clings so closely, and let us run with perseverance the race that is set before us, looking to Jesus the pioneer and perfecter of our faith, who for the sake of the joy that was set before him endured the cross, disregarding its shame, and has taken his seat at the right hand of the throne of God.

—HEBREWS 12:1–2

Outside Caen in the Normandy countryside of France is a little cemetery. Atop one of the graves is a cross on which is etched these words: "Leadership is wisdom and courage and a great carelessness of self." Which means, of course, that leaders must from time to time put to hazard their own political future in order to do what is right in the long-term interests of those they have by solemn oath sworn to serve. Easy to say. Tough to do.[15]

If we are genuinely faithful leaders, there comes (or will come) a time in our careers when we must practice "a great carelessness of self." It is a time when we must fly in the face of personal expediency in order to be faithful to the long-term interests of our organizations—and to God. We let go of our personal agendas, our career paths, our political and social connections, to do the right thing by God. The religious word for practicing a great carelessness of self is "sacrifice."

But when the time for sacrifice comes, we are not alone. We are surrounded on every side by a great cloud of witnesses, those who have gone before us. Out of faithfulness, each practiced that great carelessness of self, regardless of immediate reward or success. These witnesses who surround and strengthen us are not only the famous and successful, like King David, Samuel, and the prophets; these witnesses, as Paul writes, "through faith conquered kingdoms, administered justice, obtained promises, shut the mouths of lions, quenched raging fires, escaped the edge of the sword, won strength out of weakness, became mighty in war, [and] put foreign armies to flight." We are also accompanied by those unknown, who did not live to see the results of their sacrifice— "they were stoned to death, they were sawn in two, they were killed by the sword; they went about in the skins of sheep and goats, destitute, persecuted, tormented—of whom the world was not worthy. They wandered in deserts and mountains, and in caves and holes in the ground."

Sacrifice is never easy. And because our sacrifice is for the long-term good of our organizations, rarely will we see the reward. But when, out of love, faithfulness, and the joy set before us, we practice that great carelessness of self, we never sacrifice alone. The cloud of witnesses who surround us will carry us through heaven's gate.

> *Build up in me wisdom and courage, O Lord, that, when the time comes, I may practice great carelessness of self for the sake of my organization. Amen.*

Meaningful Delegation

These twelve Jesus sent out with the following instructions: "Go nowhere among the Gentiles, and enter no town of the Samaritans, but go rather to the lost sheep of the house of Israel. As you go, proclaim the good news, 'The kingdom of heaven has come near.' Cure the sick, raise the dead, cleanse the lepers, cast out demons. You received without payment; give without payment."

—MATTHEW 10:5–8

To be a good leader and a poor delegator is a contradiction in terms. Delegation is one of the ways for a leader to connect voice and touch. It is a precious way of enabling people to participate, to grow, to reach toward their potential. It is the best process for personal development because it gives people the opportunity to learn by doing, to take risks, and to become comfortable with the consequences of their own performance.[16]

Good leaders delegate. It is how we learn what's really happening in our organizations, with our constituents and customers. It's also how we retain and grow our best employees.

My boss delegates tasks to me frequently. But she is thoughtful about what kinds of jobs she delegates to me. There are things she needs me to help her with that just need to be done—"housekeeping" tasks that keep the business going. She also makes sure, however, that mixed among the housekeeping chores are jobs that really contribute to the success of the company, raise my visibility in the organization, and give me some real responsibility that can bring real rewards. In other words, my boss makes sure she also delegates meaningful work to me.

Handing off "grunt work" isn't delegation. Good leaders delegate work that gives their staff responsibility, a chance to make significant contributions to the organization and reap the rewards. Not every job we delegate needs to be meaningful, but if we want to keep and grow our best employees, we must make sure that we give them important work in which they can take pride and be responsible.

One of the things Jesus was really good at was delegation. He delegated to his disciples nothing less than the proclamation of the kingdom of God. It was a tough job that carried enormous responsibility. And the reward? The kingdom of heaven. Jesus wasn't afraid of mistakes his disciples would make as they went about their work. The disciples were imperfect delegates, but they grew into their jobs. And as they grew and learned from their mistakes, the gospel was preached—and the church grew throughout the world.

Delegating meaningful work to our staff is an act of faith in which God is at work. And as our employees reach their potential, so will our organizations.

> *God, give me the courage today to delegate important work to my best people. Amen.*

Risk Losing It

Yet whatever gains I had, these I have come to regard as loss because of Christ. More than that, I regard everything as loss because of the surpassing value of knowing Christ Jesus my Lord. For his sake I have suffered the loss of all things, and I regard them as rubbish, in order that I may gain Christ and be found in him, not having a righteousness of my own that comes from the law, but one that comes through faith in Christ, the righteousness from God based on faith.

—PHILIPPIANS 3:7–9

Nevertheless, it's important that we fail. We need to fail often. If we don't, it means we're not testing our limits. It means we're not taking the necessary risks to improve our behavior. Tennis players who never double-fault are playing the game too cautiously. Skiers who never fall are not skiing close to their capabilities. But we don't learn from those failure experiences.[17]

There is a paradox to leadership: leaders are supposed to be risk takers, but leaders are not supposed to fail. Yet risk *isn't* risk unless the possibility, even probability, of failure is very great. But leaders are supposed to fail, and we are to learn from those failure experiences. That is how we expand our skills, capabilities, and competencies. We don't grow as leaders by playing it safe, by staying in our personal comfort zones. The problem is, we don't learn from our failures, we learn from our successes. Too often, we stay in our comfort zone believing that "what worked once must always work," and we rarely risk failing to discover new talents, hone our expertise, or enhance our flair for leadership.

There is a paradox to Christian faith. When we fail, we cannot fail, for we lose all to find Christ. J.R.R. Tolkien, author of the epic adventure fantasy *Lord of the Rings*, once wrote that there is no adventure without the real threat of failure. As Christian leaders, we are on a great adventure of faith in which we are called to risk failure at almost every turn. There is no comfort zone. In fact, we are to count our successes as losses if our successes don't bring us closer to Christ. We risk everything every day to know and be found in Christ—not having a righteousness built from a string of countless successes, but having a righteousness built exclusively on faith in Christ's grace. As Christian leaders, we are called to risk and to fail often—and to learn and grow from failure, to go beyond our limits and expand our abilities to serve better our organizations and God. For when we fail, we fall into the loving arms of Christ, who alone sustains us and the organizations we lead.

Let me fail boldly, O Christ, in the right things, that I may grow into being the leader you want me to be. Amen.

Community: A Kind of Love

> If then there is any encouragement in Christ, any
> consolation from love, any sharing in the Spirit, any com-
> passion and sympathy, make my joy complete: be of the
> same mind, having the same love, being in full accord and
> of one mind. Do nothing from selfish ambition or con-
> ceit, but in humility regard others as better than your-
> selves. Let each of you look not to your own interests, but
> to the interest of others.
>
> —PHILIPPIANS 2:1–4

> [Love] is a word that does not often arise in con-
> versations about management development, yet
> love is fundamental to good leadership, because
> leadership is about caring. Indeed, caring is the
> basis for community, and the first job of the leader
> is to build community, a deep feeling of unity, a fel-
> lowship.[18]

A colleague returned recently from a month-
long vacation with her family in Europe. Her
first day back in the office, she exclaimed, "I'm so
happy to be back in my community!" This from
an intelligent woman with a rich and happy home
life, a woman who is very active in her local
church. Yet she identifies her colleagues and team-
mates at work as her community. I was surprised,

and flattered, by the power of her statement because basically she was telling us how much she loved us.

At the end of the day, leadership is all about love. Our first job as leaders, especially Christian leaders, is to build community in our organizations. And community is built on genuine caring, genuine love for one another. And the recipe for building community based on love is found in Paul's letter to the Philippians: "Let each of you look not to your own interests, but to the interests of others." That is how love looks in community. That is how we lead. We create an organization in which each person looks to the interests of others—other employees, customers, and constituents. And they learn to do this by watching us, experiencing our genuine care and concern for the whole organization expressed through service. As leaders, we do nothing from selfish ambition or conceit, but in humility we regard others as better than ourselves—out of love.

> *I love my organization, O Lord. Help me to love it even more. Amen.*

The Art of
Systematic Neglect

But [Elijah] went a day's journey into the wilderness, and
came and sat down under a solitary broom tree. He asked
that he might die: "It is enough; now, O Lord, take away
my life, for I am no better than my ancestors."
—1 KINGS 19:4

The ability to withdraw and reorient oneself, if
only for a moment, presumes that [the leader] has
learned the art of systematic neglect, to sort out the
more important from the less important—and the
important from the urgent—and attend to the
more important, even though there may be penal-
ties and censure for the neglect of something else.
One may govern one's life by the optimum (optimum being that pace and set of choices that give
one the best performance over a lifespan), bearing
in mind that there are always emergencies and that
the optimum includes carrying an unused reserve
of energy in all periods of normal demand so that
one has the resilience to cope with the emergency.[19]

Elijah the prophet, fearing Jezebel's threats,
flees for his life into the wilderness and sits
down exhausted under a broom tree. There he
begged God to take his life because he was no bet-

ter, no more special, than any of his ancestors. Now this is a man who had been fed by God's hand during famine and drought, healed a widow's son from a life-threatening illness, and watched the fire of God burn up the offerings of pagan priests of Baal. Elijah had lost all perspective about who he was. And he had been so busy being a prophet that he exhausted himself of all energy and had no more resilience to cope with the present emergency—Jezebel.

As leaders, our responsibilities and hours can be grueling. After a series of twelve-hour days coping with several emergencies, it's easy to get run down and sloppy in our work. To recharge our batteries, we've got to practice regularly the art of systematic neglect, the discipline of solitude.

After battling Jezebel's priests, Elijah was in no condition for an encounter with God; he had no energy left to hear God's voice. Had Elijah not fled into the wilderness, he would not have encountered God's angel, who helped him refuel for his meeting with God in the cave. We can't afford to get so tired and depleted that we miss God. Getting away by ourselves regularly, even if it's only for a little while, gives us the opportunity to sort out priorities and make decisions about what we can and cannot do. And there is time for solitude—when we have the courage to neglect some items on our agenda in order to recharge and get energized for more important items.

When we practice systematic neglect regularly, we can better cope with the priorities and emergencies of our organizations.

> *Give me the energy I need today, O Lord, to serve you and my organization by coping with what's really important. Amen.*

Why Lead?

For God is my witness, how I long for all of you with the compassion of Christ Jesus. And this is my prayer, that your love may overflow more and more with knowledge and full insight to help you determine what is best, so that in the day of Christ you may be pure and blameless, having the harvest of righteousness that comes through Jesus Christ for the glory and praise of God.

—PHILIPPIANS 1:8–11

Let me close with a fundamental question—so basic that you almost never hear it asked: Why would anyone even want to be a leader today? In times past, the reasons were pretty obvious: you wanted . . . power; it meant control over others; it meant being served. . . . But today, . . . the power of leaders is diffuse. Leaders themselves have many constituencies to answer to, and the people they lead are better informed, more questioning, and far less obedient. There have to be different motives for leadership. . . . Today's leaders . . . want to help others realize their own power and dignity. They lead because they want to create an environment in which people are free to think, innovate, and unite into teams and groups, in order to solve problems that are too big for any one person to solve alone.[20]

Why do we want to lead? What motivates us? What is it about being a leader that gives us joy? These are questions we must ask ourselves, not just once, but regularly throughout our careers. Over the years, we change and grow as leaders. It helps to set aside times for regular reflection on our motivation for leadership.

The answer to these questions for the Apostle Paul is most likely found in the opening of his letter to the Philippians: he leads because he loves. The power of Paul's love for the Philippians is deep and joyous. He leads so that their "love may overflow more and more with knowledge a full insight" so that Christ will find them pure and blameless. Paul leads because he wants to help the Philippians "realize their own power and dignity" in love before God.

For us, there are no "right" answers to these questions, there are only honest ones. The answers we give will tell us a lot about ourselves and our relationship with God. Our answers will prompt more questions: Is this the kind of leader God wants me to be? What is it and who is it I really love about my job? As a disciple of Christ, how do I treat my followers? What does my motivation for leadership tell me about my relationship with God? Does my leadership style give me a real, lasting, deep joy, the kind that Paul has when he writes to his beloved Philippians?

Understanding our motivation to lead can help us be better servants and stewards of those God has given us to lead—and deepen our relationship with God who calls us.

> *Help me to understand better why I lead,*
> *O Lord, so that I may serve you better.*
> *Amen.*

Only One Thing

> [Martha] had a sister named Mary, who sat at the Lord's feet and listened to what he was saying. But Martha was distracted by her many tasks; so she came to him and asked, "Lord, do you not care that my sister has left me to do all the work by myself? Tell her then to help me." But the Lord answered her, "Martha, Martha, you are worried and distracted by many things; there is need of only one thing. Mary has chosen the better part, which will not be taken away from her."
>
> —LUKE 10:39–42

> If there is any one "secret" of effectiveness, it is concentration. Effective executives do first things first and they do one thing at a time. . . . Concentration—that is, the courage to impose on time and events his own decision as to what really matters and comes first—is the executive's only hope of becoming the master of time and events instead of their whipping boy.[21]

Most leaders tend to be Marthas. We are worried and distracted by many things. A wide variety of constituencies—employees, customers, vendors, board members, analysts, bankers—demand our attention. We have a lot—sometimes a crushing amount—of responsibility on our shoulders. We're very busy. Our time is precious and scarce. Yet effective leaders are Marys—they concentrate on only one thing at a time.

The new CEO at our company is a typical Martha. He has sixteen direct reports—a leadership team that is fragmented and fractious and not very competent. Because the CEO was promoted from within, he has lots of old, personal loyalties across the organization, people who demand special treatment. The company is in a "turnaround," and the financial situation is dire. Employees are terrified of losing their jobs, and they demand answers about their futures *now*. The poor man has good reason to be worried and distracted by many things. Yet what our company needs desperately is for the CEO to concentrate. We really need him to *lead;* we need him to have "the courage to impose on time and events his own decision as to what really matters and comes first"—and act on it. Strange as it seems, most of the employees at our company are longing to be told "no" to their conflicting special interests so that the CEO can concentrate on one thing at a time and begin to lead us out of this mess.

"Lord, do you not care that my sister has left me to do all the work by myself?" is Martha's heartfelt plea to Jesus. But Jesus has not left us leaders alone to do all the work by ourselves. Other leaders in our organization are ready to help us; we can enlist the hearts, minds, and hands of our employees. When we do, we free ourselves up to concentrate on that which will have the biggest impact on our organizations. When we do, we can concentrate on what's most important—and then we can truly *lead*.

> *Show me, Lord, what is the most important, single thing to concentrate on in my organization. Amen.*

Build a Foundation

Everyone then who hears these words of mine and acts on them will be like a wise man who built his house on rock. The rain fell, the floods came, and the winds blew and beat on that house, but it did not fall, because it had been founded on rock.

—MATTHEW 7:24–25

It isn't necessary to choose between action and spirituality. . . . Our spirituality, our centeredness, is a vital and strong support for the many difficulties encountered in the active function of leadership. In a world where change is so rapid that what we have learned today may be inaccurate tomorrow, a balance of spirit, action, and faith in those around us is essential.[22]

I know a leader whose nonprofit organization is going through a funding crisis that will require her to reorganize and downsize her staff. The crisis has paralyzed her. She is literally flailing about as she tries to figure out alternatives to "right sizing." Because she has a great need to be liked, and many of her direct reports are close friends, she's afraid that the reorganization will cost her friendships. And so she delays taking action while her board and other constituents grow more and more frustrated with her. Unfortunately, this leader has no "rock," no intentional, spiritual foundation upon which to weather such an organizational storm.

The early monastics, like Saint Benedict, wrote spiritual "rules" to live by for themselves and their communities. Rules like Benedict's, recorded very simply how the monks were to live daily with God and with each other. In anticipation of our own organizational storms, we leaders can create our own spiritual rule, based on Christ's gospel, to help us build a spiritual foundation and discipline that will support us when the going gets tough. Try creating your own rule in a journal or notebook:

- In writing, set aside regular times to pray for your organization. Make a simple list of people and needs to pray about. Select Bible passages to read and meditate on.
- Establish a few foundational guidelines or principles to follow about how you believe God wants you to interact with the people in your organization. How does God want you to behave toward them, especially during tough times?
- Write how you understand God's call to leadership. What is it God is calling you to do as a leader now? How has that call changed? What has stayed the same? What does this mean for your organization?

- Identify other believers outside your organization who will pray for you and support you.

> *Help me to build my house on the rock of your words, O Lord, that I may serve you well. Amen.*

Strong Statements

When the days came near for him to be taken up, he set his face to go to Jerusalem.

—LUKE 9:51

Hap Klopp, president of North Face, the world's leading manufacturer of outdoor adventure equipment, has observed: "Every decision is a statement, even those decisions you don't intend as such. Some are statements to the masses. Some are statements to a few. All are statements to and about yourself." . . . It is very important to understand the importance of every decision you make as a leader. Each decision will affect people, it will communicate your values, it will symbolize your understanding of the whole and your willingness to share or clutch power. It will serve as the strongest indicator of your respect for the expertise among your team members.[23]

There is a leader in our company who is famous for being indecisive. It amazes many people that he got to be a leader at all. He'll do anything rather than decide; he talks all around a decision. He consults and consults, he builds continual consensus, he researches endlessly. What this leader understands intuitively is that decisions disclose who we really are as leaders, and he doesn't want to make any self-revealing statements.

Jesus made a decision that spoke volumes about who he was and his mission: "He set his face to go to Jerusalem." Jesus decided to go to the very place that would lead to his death and, ultimately, his resurrection. His decision to head toward Jerusalem encapsulates the gospel—that God's Son came to die so that all may have eternal life. It was a decision that stated God's great and terrible love for humanity; it was a decision that stated that the Christian journey requires great sacrifice to experience great joy; it was a decision that stated Jesus' understanding of himself as the Messiah.

The decisions we make as leaders speak volumes about who we are to our organizations and our mission. Not all decisions we make are equally important or have equal impact. But taken as a whole, our decisions can give us the gift of awareness; our decisions tell us about ourselves and tell others about us. They can teach us a lot about ourselves and how we are shaping our organizations through our leadership. They can teach us about our values, how we understand our organization, and how we really feel about holding and sharing power. They can teach us about how we serve God as leaders.

> *May I learn more about how I lead from the decisions I make today, O Lord. Amen.*

The Power of Relationships

Now before the festival of the Passover, Jesus knew that his hour had come to depart from this world and go to the Father. Having loved his own who were in the world, he loved them to the end.

—JOHN 13:1

Even organizational power is surely relational. One evening, I had a long exploratory talk with a wise friend who told me that "power in organizations is the capacity generated by relationships." It is energy that comes into existence through relationships. Ever since that conversation, I have changed what I pay attention to in an organization. Now I look carefully at a workplace's capacity for healthy relationships. . . . Do people know how to listen and speak to each other? To work well with diverse members? Do people have free access to one another throughout the organization? Are they trusted with open information? . . . Can people speak truthfully to one another?[24]

It helps the job of being a leader tremendously if we are "people people"—that, fundamentally, we like people and are interested in them. So much of leadership is relationship management—

helping the people in our organizations work well together to achieve organizational success. Organizational power *is* relational. And liking, or at least respecting, the people we lead energizes us for our jobs as leaders.

What comes through the gospels again and again is how much Jesus loved people and was genuinely interested in them. He loved his own and he loved them to the end. And the love and interest Jesus showed people laid the foundation for one of the greatest organizations in the world—the church.

My present boss is a woman who genuinely likes people—all kinds of people. She is fascinated by why people do the things they do and how she can help the people that work for her grow and develop on the job. It's so easy to do my best work for someone who really likes me and respects what I do. Most of us have probably had bosses at one time or other who were either uninterested in us at best or actively disliked us and our work—and we remember how agonizing is was to really do our best in that kind of relationship.

When we like and respect the people in our organizations, people tend to listen and speak to each other, many different kinds of people work well together, there is more access to people and information across the organization, and people can speak the truth to one another. So it helps our organizations for us leaders to reflect on what it is we like about the people we work with—and to thank God for them.

> *Thank you, O God, for the people you have called to work in my organization. Amen.*

Out of Control

Do not fret because of the wicked;
do not be envious of wrongdoers,
for they will soon fade like the grass,
and wither like the green herb.
Trust in the Lord, and do good;
so you will live in the land, and enjoy security.
Take delight in the Lord,
and he will give you the desires of your heart.

—PSALM 17:1–4

I have given up trying to control anything. It has
taken me a long while to learn this, but I finally
understand that the universe refuses to cooperate
with my desire to play God.[25]

Giving up the desire to control is a lesson we
leaders must learn often. After all, we're
doers; we take action; we take control almost naturally. But our organizations have a life of their
own because they are made up of complicated
human beings working together in a web of complex relationships. It is impossible to be completely
in control of such a complex organism. Trying to
do so will only make us crazy—and take a lot of
the joy out of being leaders.

Annie Dillard once wrote that anyone who thinks they're in control is asleep at the switch. A Christian leader who wants to control every aspect of her organization is an oxymoron. Faith is not about control. In fact, faith is about giving up control. It's about elegant surrender to God, who is good. We are servants—not controllers—of our organizations. We are servants—not gods—of our God, who wants the very best for us and our organizations. Fretting and worrying over those things that are not under our control is not only pointless, it's also faithless. Our jobs as leaders is to do the very best we can—to trust in the Lord and do good. For the God we trust is the God who wants to give us the desires of our hearts.

Lord, help me to resist the temptation to be totally in control today. Amen.

Get Outside

Now those who were scattered went from place to place, proclaiming the word.

—ACTS 8:4

For the executive there is, in the end, only one way to get [meaningful outside information]: that is to *go, personally, on the outside*. No matter how good the reports, no matter how good the economic or financial theory underlying them, nothing beats personal, direct observation, and in a form that is truly *outside* observation. English supermarket chains have again and again tried to establish themselves in neighboring Ireland—with very little success. The leading supermarket chain in Ireland is Super-Quinn, started and run by Fergal Quinn. His secret is not better merchandise or lower prices. His secret is that he and all of his company's executives have to spend two days a week outside their offices. One day is spent actually doing a job in a supermarket. . . . And one day is spent in competitors' stores watching, listening, talking to the competitors' employees and the competitors' customers.[26]

When I was marketing manager for a large specialty retail chain, the most valuable—and memorable—days I spent were working in the stores as a clerk. I didn't sell a lot of merchandise, but I watched carefully how our customers shopped, and talked with a lot of them about what they liked and didn't like about their shopping experience. When it came time to design the next promotion or marketing campaign, I was fully armed with the knowledge of what our customers found valuable—and could tailor my work to meet their needs. Perhaps even more valuable for me was just getting out of the office and concentrating on how the world works for a little while. It made my work so much more meaningful and genuinely helpful to the company and our customers. And I enjoyed myself thoroughly.

A leader is involved personally—not only within her organization, but also with those outside of it. What if Saul had stayed in Damascus after his conversion to Christianity, or Philip had remained in Jerusalem ministering to the saints, or Jesus had confined himself to Galilee? How different our world today would be! If through our leadership we want to change our world, we've got to get out and actually talk to customers, constituents, vendors, and competitors. We've got to have personal, unmediated contact with them. Paul, Philip, Peter, Barnabas, Timothy, and countless others unnamed traveled the ancient world to bring the gospel to people who desperately wanted to hear the word of God. Some of these leaders wrote about God in letters—but all of them went to see for themselves what was going on in the world and to tell people about God *personally*. As leaders, we can't afford not to have the time to meet personally with people on the outside—the very reasons our organizations exist in the first place.

> *Lord, lead me outside my organization so that I may become a better leader. Amen.*

The Second Half

O God, from my youth you have taught me,
and I still proclaim your wondrous deeds.
So even to old age and gray hairs,
O God, do not forsake me,
until I proclaim your might to all the generations
    to come.
Your power and your righteousness, O God
reach the high heavens.

—PSALM 7:17–19

What to do with the second half of one's life? . . . There
is a great deal of talk today about the "mid-life crisis" of the executive. It is mostly boredom. At age
forty-five, most executives have reached the peak of
their business career and know it. After twenty
years of doing very much the same kind of work,
they are good at their jobs. But few are learning
anything anymore, few are contributing anything
anymore and few expect the job again to become a
challenge and a satisfaction. . . . To manage oneself,
therefore, will increasingly require preparing oneself for the second half of one's life.[27]

There is a second half to our lives as leaders.
Just as we'd be negligent if we didn't make
plans for our organizations, we'd be equally

negligent should we not make plans for what we want to do after our present careers end. At middle age we need to consider what it is we want to do with the rest of our lives. We need to figure out how we can serve God with the second half of our lives.

Peter Drucker outlines three answers to the question he poses: *What to do with the second half of one's life?* We can get retrained or reeducated in order to begin a second career; we can work on developing a parallel career while still employed in our present jobs; we can work as "social entrepreneurs," either paid or volunteer, usually in a nonprofit environment. I chose to develop a parallel career. As I built my career in the first half of my life, I became a skilled writer and discovered how much I enjoyed it. I began to take on projects and jobs in my daily work that required a lot of writing or editing. Eventually, I scaled back on management jobs until I was able to take my present job in which writing is my primary responsibility. At the same time and outside of my day job, I began to write and publish steadily, using weekends, holidays, and vacations in which to write. I still have my day job, but I've acquired enough experience and enough of a portfolio so that in a few years I'll be able to "semiretire" as a full-time writer and editor on my own.

Just because we're middle-aged, a little bored, or suffering from "executive mid-life crisis" doesn't mean God is through with us yet. Our job is to plan and prepare for the second half.

> *Show me how I can serve you, Lord, with the second half of my life. Amen.*

The Secret Is Enough

Bless those who persecute you; bless and do not curse
them. Rejoice with those who rejoice, weep with those
who weep. Live in harmony with one another; do not be
haughty, associate with the lowly; do not claim to be wiser
than you are. Do not repay anyone evil for evil, but take
thought for what is noble in the sight of all. If it is possible, so far as it depends on you, live peaceably with all.

—ROMANS 12:14–18

Abundance mentality—a bone-deep belief that
"there are enough natural and human resources to
realize my dream" and that "my success does not
necessarily mean failure for others, just as their
success does not necessarily preclude my own."
Over the past twenty-five years of working with
organizations and with individuals, I have observed
that the abundance mentality often makes the difference between excellence and mediocrity, particularly because it eliminates small thinking and
adversarial relations.[28]

Too often organizations—and those who lead
them—function on the myth of scarcity. The
myth of scarcity says, "I've got to get mine while

the getting's still good, and the rest of you can go to a very warm, very bad place." We've all watched people climb our organizations' leadership ranks, clinging to the myth of scarcity. The problem with the myth of scarcity is that it works for some individuals. The problem with the myth of scarcity is that it doesn't work well in the long term for organizational success.

Now, we've all got to lead and work in organizations with dwindling budgets and finite human talent. But the secret to long-term success for our organizations as a whole is the firm belief that *there is enough and more than enough* for all of us to succeed together. Financial and human resources may be finite, but there is enough for us to be successful when we work well together.

The belief that there is enough and more than enough is a spiritual principle. When we all feel that we have enough, we can live in peace with others and with our God. Because we always have enough, no one can take anything away from us, and we can go the extra mile with people: we can bless those who bad-mouth us, and we can rejoice over the successes of others and genuinely weep with those who've experienced failure or tragedy. We are careless of status, careless of what others think of us. When we believe we have enough and more than enough, we live in harmony with others in our organizations and are free to work through problems with them peaceably to accomplish our mutual goals. And that adds up to long-term success for our communities, our organizations.

> *Lord, today there is enough and more than enough for me to get the job done with others. Amen.*

A Voice from Outside

> Yet he sent prophets among them to bring them back to the Lord; they testified against them, but they would not listen.
>
> —2 CHRONICLES 24:19

In the 1980s, Verne Moreland, then an executive at NCR, half-facetiously proposed that companies appoint one individual to function in the role [the] "fool" used to play in royal courts. The official corporate fool would be given license to "disturb with glimpses of confounding truth, . . . to challenge by jest and conundrum all that is sacred and all the savants have proved to be rue and immutable." In fact, Moreland anticipated the growing trend among CEOs to hire "coaches"—individuals who are not part of the regular organization and, thus, are free to tell the boss what he or she may not want to hear from subordinates.[29]

To be a leader there are some things we must give up in order to be effective. One of those things is identifying ourselves closely with a particular set or "clique" of individuals, our buddies. In other words, we don't get to hang around with our cronies all the time the way we used to.

Our CEO hasn't learned this lesson and it's hurting his ability to lead. Our company has an employee cafeteria that sells breakfast and lunch, as well as snacks, soft drinks, and coffee throughout the day. Day after day, our CEO has coffee at the same time with the same six senior executives. No one else is ever invited to join them. Later, the CEO has lunch with the same six people. Again, no one is invited to join them. What this behavior has done is to tell employees that their CEO isn't interested in them, their work, or what they might be thinking or feeling about how we're getting our company out of financial trouble. Employees speculate that these same six executives must tell the CEO exactly what he wants to hear, or he'd be out circulating among a lot of other different people to get a fix on how the company is doing.

Sometimes we leaders need prophets to keep us honest and growing into being the kind of leader God wants us to be. It is my fondest wish that if our CEO absolutely must hang out with his cronies all day, he would at least hire a corporate prophet, or "fool"—a coach that would give him honest, constructive feedback about his leadership skills and abilities. That prophetic voice from the outside can help our CEO, or any of us, when we get too insulated from our organizations, to hear and live the truth about ourselves as leaders and about our organizations. And when we hear the truth God wants us to hear from a corporate prophet, for heaven's sake, let's not make him our new buddy.

> *O Lord, send me one of your prophets so that I might hear your truth. Amen.*

A Few Simple Words

No one can say "Jesus is Lord" except by the Holy
Spirit.

—1 CORINTHIANS 12:3

Sam Walton, Herb Kelleher, and other effective
leaders disciplined themselves to make things so
simple that their followers would never be con-
fused about what they should be doing and why.
That Wal-Mart is dedicated to "low prices and
good service" and that Southwest's employees
should "make flying fun" are messages so simple
that they cannot be further reduced. . . . Simplistic,
ritualistic, and formulaic statements by leaders
aren't worth rotten fruit on a tree, but the ability to
present an unadorned idea that compels action is
the greatest gift of leadership.[30]

It takes hard work to "present an unadorned idea
that compels action." It takes a lot of thought
and discussion to boil down into very few words
what it is we want our organizations to do. When
I worked for a large bank, the CEO came up with
a motto for all employees at all levels of management. After a lot of thought and talk with staff
members throughout the bank, he said that we

would be "the best place to bank, the best place to work, and the best place to invest." Every action he or his leadership took had to have a visible connection with that motto. And it worked—because all of us employees really wanted to bank, work, and invest in the best bank in the country. Our CEO's motto compelled action.

Almost two thousand years ago, another motto compelled action among people in an organization: "Jesus is Lord." This simple phrase was said at conversions and baptisms, and when individuals identified themselves as Christians. Leaders in the early church instinctively knew the power of a simple phrase that boiled down their faith into three powerful words. So powerful was the phrase that they knew that only true believers could utter it, inspired by the Holy Spirit.

A motto or phrase that sums up our organizations' missions and compels action among employees and customers need not be an empty, mindless slogan. Like that of the early church, a meaningful, simple phrase can inspire people to dream and create, build and serve.

> *I will work hard, Lord, to create a motto that inspires my organization. Amen.*

What Do You Want to Say?

For God so loved the world that he gave his only Son, so that everyone who believes in him may not perish but may have eternal life.

—JOHN 3:16

One of the most-quoted lines [about Coca-Cola—quoting the late Roberto Goizueta, Coca-Cola's renowned leader in the 1980s and 1990s] describe[s] Coke's "infinite" growth potential: *each of the six billion people on this planet drinks, on average, sixty-four ounces of fluids daily, of which only two ounces are Coca-Cola.* . . . All leaders must spend hours identifying, refining, practicing, and internalizing the key messages they seek to convey to customers, employees, investors, dealers, and suppliers. Hollywood producers have it right: if you can't get your message across in a couple of compelling sentences, either you don't have a marketable story line or you haven't discovered it yet.[31]

Really powerful messages, messages that move people and get them to act, are hard to create. They take careful thought and construction. Perhaps the hardest part is figuring out exactly what it is we leaders want to say to our organizations and constituents. It's worth a lot of thought and time spent talking to trusted others to figure out what it is we want to say. Then, once we know what our message is, we need to get to work on making it brief, simple, and memorable. Is the message compelling enough? Will it inspire people to behave differently? Will it, like Goizueta's message, "wow" them into action? It's not just a form of advertising; it's good, solid communication—communication that effects real, positive change in our organizations.

Look at John 3:16. It is, arguably, the summation of the entire Gospel. If we had nothing else—no other text but John 3:16, the Gospel would still be communicated in its entirety, and we would still fall on our knees. *One sentence* can have incredible power—power for good, power to effect real change in minds, hearts, and spirits. The writer of John wasn't advertising; he was letting God speak through him—simply, with power and grace. And the effect is a sentence that has brought untold generations into God's kingdom.

Finding out what we want to say, and then crafting a simple, powerful message for our organizations, is part of what being a leader is all about. It's the least we can do.

Lord, help me to know what I really want to say, and give me the skills to craft a powerful message. Amen.

Transforming Leadership

> Pursue peace with everyone, and the holiness without which no one will see the Lord. See to it that no one fails to obtain the grace of God; that no root of bitterness springs up and causes trouble, and through it many become defiled.
>
> —HEBREWS 12:14–15

> [Transforming] leadership occurs when one or more persons *engage* with others in such a way that leaders and followers raise one another to higher levels of motivation and morality. . . . Their purposes, which might have started out as separate but related . . . become fused. Power bases are linked not as counterweights but as mutual support for common purpose. . . . Transforming leadership ultimately becomes *moral* in that it raises the level of human conduct and ethical aspiration of both leader and the led, and thus it has a transforming effect on both.[32]

I once worked for a company that made products to help people better understand, appreciate, and enjoy nature. By the time I came to work there, the company had grown quite large, and Tom, the company's founder, had died a few years prior. I remember talking to employees who had joined the firm when it was young and worked directly for Tom. Workers' eyes would light up when they talked about working for him. Tom's passion for the natural world was infectious, and each encounter with his staff was an opportunity to share his passion individually. When he looked at his employees, he saw the hope and future of the world's environment. Employees told me how much knowing and working for Tom had transformed their lives.

How would our leadership be transformed if we saw Christ in those we work with? A "transformed leader" is one who constantly pursues the peace of Christ with everyone in his or her organization. To look for Christ among our employees certainly "raises the level of human conduct and ethical aspiration of both the leader and the led." To pursue the peace of Christ among those with whom we work transforms us and our coworkers; it infuses our leadership and work with a deep passion, a passion that is infectious. It's not about preaching to our organizations, it's about serving them, even loving them. When we serve the people of our organizations as though they were Christ, we pursue a holiness without which no one will see the Lord, and we raise the ethical and moral bar of our organizations, which become places where people are eager to work and serve and are passionate about what they do. To find

Christ in our employees is to see the future and hope of our world.

> *May I find you, O Christ, in everyone I touch today. Amen.*

The
Leadership
Vision

The Vision Business

> Then Solomon said, "The LORD has said that he would reside in thick darkness. I have built you an exalted house, a place for you to reside in forever. . . . My father David had it in mind to build a house or the name of the LORD, the God of Israel. . . . Now the LORD has fulfilled his promise that he made, for I have succeeded my father David, and sit on the throne of Israel, as the LORD promised, and have built the house for the name of the LORD, the God of Israel."
>
> —2 CHRONICLES 6:1–2, 7, 10

> Making life better in the long run is a key element in getting extraordinary things done. . . . Without vision, little could happen. All enterprises or projects, big or small, begin in the mind's eye; they begin with imagination and with the belief that what's merely an image can one day be made real.[1]

I've got vision," Butch Cassidy exclaimed, "and the rest of the world's wearing bifocals." Some of the great leaders in the Bible—David, Moses, Deborah the judge, Isaiah, Anna the prophetess, Paul—must have felt like Butch Cassidy sometimes. They had visions of what their worlds could become long before they saw their visions realized. And they were willing to move heaven and earth to see their visions take shape—visions of hope and promises of God's love and mercy. But those visions were not always welcomed or greeted with enthusiasm—because often those visions challenged the status quo and turned the world on its collective ear.

A leader's job is to have vision—and to move heaven and earth to make it so. We're supposed to make life better, or at least more successful, for the people in our organizations—sometimes in spite of themselves. And that can't happen without imagination and commitment. We not only have to be able to see in our mind's eye where our organizations are going, we've also got to have the commitment necessary to make our vision become reality. Not everybody in our organizations will welcome our visions. So we take a page from one of the Bible's leaders—we inspire, cajole, threaten, make predictions, listen, yell, share, give orders, and love (always love)—to make our world a better place.

> *May my vision find honor with you, O God, and may I have the strength and commitment I need to see it come true. Amen.*

Leadership as Art

> I, Daniel, alone saw the vision; the people who were with me did not see the vision, though a great trembling fell upon them, and they fled and hid themselves. So I was left alone to see this great vision.
>
> —DANIEL 10:7–8

We also suggest that a desire for leadership must be part of a broader personal vision. Without internal clarity about what you want for your life, your leadership will lack clear purpose, and you may find yourself leading others to a place you don't necessarily want to go. Leadership can be an instrument of personal expression that enriches your choice of trade, specialty, or vocation. Leadership can also be a vehicle a person can use to help accomplish a personal vision. If a particular leadership job or role does not foster and enhance the agendas of your personal vision, then perhaps you should either look for a leadership role that will or else say no to leadership at this time.[2]

Leadership is an art. And like art, leadership is a form of self-expression; the best leaders lead from a very personal place deep in themselves. Leadership is a personal, as well as professional, passion.

Therefore, it's critical for those of us who lead to know clearly what it is we want to do with our lives personally, as well as know what drives us and what we feel most passionately about, and we must make sure that our personal vision aligns with the organizations we lead. And should our personal vision disconnect from our organizations when, like Daniel, our personal vision isn't shared with others, we must have the courage to leave, be alone with our vision for a while, and reassess how God may be calling us to leadership.

Jane was one of the few women senior ministers of a "megachurch." She had spent more than a decade building her church into a large, very successful organization. She began to feel that the excitement and passion that led her into the ministry had evaporated over the last few years. The bigger the church grew, the more disengaged Jane became. She took a leave of absence from her congregation to do some soul searching. She discovered that her personal vision, her life's work, was to build churches. She was most engaged when she could experience God working through her as a "congregational architect." Jane realized that her personal vision as God's architect no longer aligned with the congregation she was currently leading. And she left to take a position at a much smaller church in rural northern Washington state.

THE LEADERSHIP VISION

> *Give me the courage to search my soul, O God, and explore my passion for leadership. Amen.*

Thinking Outside the Box

Now we have received not the spirit of the world, but the spirit that is from God, so that we may understand the gifts bestowed on us by God. And we speak of these things in words not taught by human wisdom but taught by the Spirit, interpreting spiritual things to those who are spiritual. . . . We have the mind of Christ.

—1 Corinthians 2:12–13 and 16b

You may have heard the story about a little boy's advice to the authorities who were unable to free an oversized truck that had become wedged under a low bridge. The lad surveyed the situation and then made the sensible (and obvious) suggestion that they could lower the truck by letting some air out of the tires. As the little boy proved, the invisible obvious can be made visible by anyone. It is often the most valuable service one can offer an organization. But it requires nontraditional thinking. Deeply held ideologies and cultural values, tunnel vision, selective perception, deference to the judgment of others—these are all enemies in our efforts to see what is really going on. And when the invisible obvious is pointed out to us, we are likely to have one of two reactions: Either we will reject and ignore it, or, more likely, we will simply say,

"Of course!" thinking we surely must have known it all along.[3]

I am amazed by the constant presence—and expense—of outside consultants at work in corporate America. I have nothing against consultants. Consultants have a real and valuable purpose: to help companies see "the invisible obvious." In the company I work for, the new leadership team was promoted from within. Unfortunately, many of them have spent most of their careers at this company, and they perpetuate a lot of the deeply held ideologies and cultural values, tunnel vision, and selective perception that got the company in such bad financial trouble in the first place. As a result, our parent company has sent in a bevy of highly paid consultants to tell our leadership how to fix their own business. These consultants are like the little boy giving advice to the authorities: they are pointing out the invisible obvious because our leaders are unable to render this service to the company.

Nontraditional thinking, the ability to see the invisible obvious and take action on it, is one of the most valuable services we leaders can offer our organizations. We have the mind of Christ. The Christian faith *is* nontraditional thinking. We love the unlovable, forgive sinners, find God's kingdom in small, unlikely places, discover power in weakness, experience life in death. As Christians, we already think outside the box. Our faith gives us the perspective we need to get past the appearance of things, to see the real issues and needs of our organizations, and take action. And when we can't see the invisible obvious, we have the wisdom to look for it, and reward it, among our employees—or import that insight from outside in the form of consultants or new hires.

> *Give me your mind, O Christ, that I might see the invisible obvious today.*
> *Amen.*

Creating Culture

Then they came to Capernaum; and when he was in the
house he asked them, "What were you arguing about on
the way? But they were silent, for on the way they argued
with one another who was the greatest. He sat down,
called the twelve, and said to them, "Whoever wants to
be first must be last of all and servant of all."

—MARK 9:33–35

The only thing of real importance that leaders do
is create and manage culture and . . . the unique
talent of leaders is their ability to understand and
work with culture. If one wishes to distinguish
leadership from management or administration,
one can argue that leaders create and change cultures, while managers and administrators live
within them.[4]

Jesus was a leader who created a radically different culture—a culture in which the first are last,
the poor are rich, and outsiders are insiders. He
transformed the cultural assumptions that dictate
our behavior; retribution is exchanged for forgiveness, judgment for mercy, identification with
class and caste for inclusion throughout society,

and empty religious ritual for personal and corporate sacrifice. Jesus relied on the apostles and other disciples to live within and manage the organization that embodied, and continues to embody, this cultural change: the church.

At the company where I work, our new CEO is trying to change our corporate culture. While the changes he's seeking are not nearly as vast as the kind Jesus instituted, they're pretty ambitious for us. The CEO is transforming our culture from one of entitlement to one of meritocracy, from one of rewarding employees for being nice to one of rewards based on concrete financial results, from one of endless planning and strategizing to one of execution and accomplishment, and from one that denies responsibility and blame to one of personal accountability. While he is concentrating on preaching the benefits of cultural change to our financial turnaround, he is relying on a team of managers and administrators to make those changes real.

As leaders, we change our corporate cultures to keep pace with and anticipate the changing world in which our organizations operate. We also have the vision to ensure that we have effective management that can administer the changes we make. We cannot live—and our organizations cannot succeed—without the skilled managers and administrators on our teams.

Help my managers and me to change our culture that we might better serve you. Amen.

Great Principles
Take Priority

> And [Jesus] said, "For this reason I have told you that no one can come to me unless it is granted by the Father." Because of this many of his disciples turned their back and no longer went about with him.
>
> —JOHN 6:65–66

One is bound to admire the political figure who, when great principles are at stake, has the courage to defy his constituency. Sam Houston, hero of the Texas war of independence . . ., deliberately brought an end to his political career by opposing secession. In an unforgettable warning to his fellow Southerners, he said, "Let me tell you what is coming. You may after the sacrifice of countless millions of treasure and hundreds of thousands of precious lives, as a bare possibility win Southern independence, if God be not against you. But I doubt it."[5]

Occasionally there will be times during our leadership when we must break with our followers, our constituents, for the sake of a great principle. For Jesus, that principle was his understanding of himself as God's Son—whom Jesus knew himself to be. Because he would not relent on his relationship with the Father—the very principle on which his ministry was founded—Jesus lost many followers. Breaking with much of his constituency didn't end Jesus' career—but it certainly changed it, and gave it a new, more urgent meaning.

What do we "go to the wall" for? Principles of conscience, principles of faith, principles that strike to the very heart of who we really are before God take precedence over the views and opinions our followers may have. A friend of mine is the adult education director in a large suburban church. Most of the church membership opposes abortion; my friend is pro-choice. When asked to teach a class about why Christians should be against abortion, my friend respectfully and gently declined because of his pro-choice principles. For my friend, his decision was a matter of principle, which he shared with as much love and humility as he could. While it cost him the support of some church members, many others, who could see that my friend is a man of integrity and faith, were able to respect his decision while disagreeing with him.

It's not easy to be a principled leader. Our principles will almost always exact some cost to our leadership. But our willingness to lead is also a matter of highest principle, and we gladly lead under the eye of a merciful God.

> *May I remain true to my highest principles, O Lord, even if it means breaking with those I lead. Amen.*

The Power of
Symbolic Action

Then they came to Jerusalem. And he entered the temple and began to drive out those who were selling and those who were buying in the temple, and he overturned the tables of the moneychangers and the seats of those who sold doves; and he would not allow anyone to carry anything through the temple. He was teaching and saying, "Is it not written, 'My house shall be called a house of prayer for all the nations'? But you have made it a den of robbers." And when the chief priests and the scribes heard it, they kept looking for a way to kill him; for they were afraid of him, because the whole crowd was spellbound by his teaching.

—MARK 11:15–18

Leaders use symbolic acts to communicate meaning and purpose and to unite followers around common values. . . . Merck's now-retired CEO Roy Vagelos committed that giant pharmaceutical company to giving away a drug that prevents river blindness, a disease that afflicts a million people world wide, leaving over 300,000 blind in the poorest regions of the poorest nations. The product cost Merck $200 million to develop and millions more annually to distribute free of charge to those who need it.[6]

The terrorist attack on September 11, 2001, nearly destroyed America's airline industry, which was already suffering from a prior economic slowdown. Just to stay in business, most of the major carriers were forced to lay off thousands of airline employees. CEO Leo Mullin of Delta Airlines was forced to lay off thirteen thousand employees three weeks after the tragedy. He announced that he would give up his salary for a year to help save his company and to bear a little of the burden felt by his laid-off workers. Mullin's gesture was symbolic; it showed employees and customers that he was committed to doing whatever it took to save his company.

A symbol is an external, emotional sign of a leader's internal, emotional commitment to his or her organization. Whether it's giving up a year's salary or giving away a drug to the world's poorest people, a symbolic act such as these not only shows the leader's commitment to the organization but inspires emotional commitment in employees, customers, and other constituents of the organization as well.

Jesus' actions in the temple, when coupled with his words, made a powerful symbol. His words and actions that day symbolized *free access* for any who wanted to draw near to God. To those who have been denied access because they didn't have enough money, enough power, or enough class, or weren't of the right faith, the right color, or the right gender, Jesus' actions symbolized freedom. That's what scared the chief priests and scribes, the gatekeepers: Jesus was opening up the temple to all comers. And that's what made people commit to follow Jesus that day. Jesus' symbolic actions showed them that he was committed to their freedom.

> *Help me, O God, use wisdom as I help with my organization's symbolic actions. Amen.*

The
Challenge of
Change

Change Brings New Life

> They were on the road, going up to Jerusalem, and Jesus was walking ahead of them; they were amazed, and those who followed were afraid. He took the twelve aside again and began to tell them what was to happen to him, saying, "See, we are going up to Jerusalem, and the Son of Man will be handed over to the chief priests and the scribes, and they will condemn him to death; then they will hand him over to the Gentiles; they will mock him, and spit upon him, and flog him, and kill him; and after three days he will rise again."
>
> —MARK 10:32–34

> Not to change, to stay on the path of slow death, is . . . hell. The difference is that the hell of deep change is the hero's journey. The journey puts us on a path of exhilaration, growth, and progress. The hero finds strength, power, vitality, and energy in change. In experiencing deep change, our selfishness dies.[1]

God has hardwired all of creation to change and grow. This is no less true for the journey of faith—a journey that embraces change, renewal, and resurrection in response to God's promise of new life. This doesn't mean that change and renewal is easy; it's hard work, and it often brings pain. But God's promise of resurrection gives us the strength and hope we need to make and accept change. Change brings new life. To fear the change new life brings puts resurrection at risk.

Just as new life is fundamental to God's creation, so it is to organizations as well. Markets, economic conditions, political climates—even the individual human relationships that make up our organizations—are in a constant state of flux. As leaders, to fear or deny change that brings resurrection in a rapidly changing world is to put our organizations at risk. But as people of faith, we can help our organizations through change by pointing the way toward new life made possible by change. Our organizations can experience resurrection. It is our job as their leaders, with God's help, to keep the promise alive and vital to strengthen our people for the journey through change.

> *Keep me from fearing or denying all of the changes around me, O God. Help me to see how new life can come out of all this change, and help me to keep your promise of new life visible to the people you've given me to lead. Amen.*

Opportunity in Crisis

When the Philistine [Goliath] drew nearer to meet
David, David ran quickly toward the battle line to meet
the Philistine. David put his hand in his bag, took out a
stone, slung it, and struck the Philistine on his forehead;
the stone sank into his forehead, and he fell face down on
the ground. So David prevailed over the Philistine with a
sling and a stone, striking down the Philistine and killing
him; there was no sword in David's hand.

—1 SAMUEL 17:48–50

Aides to General Dwight D. Eisenhower have
reported that at one of the most crucial moments
in World War II—in the great push across the
European theater, when it emerged that the Ger-
mans had launched the counteroffensive now
known as the "Battle of the Bulge"—Eisenhower
entered the conference with his generals with the
most remarkable attitude: this crisis was the opportunity they had needed. As Eisenhower saw it, the
German army had abandoned its defenses and
made itself vulnerable. In the face of extraordinary
danger, with German forces bearing down on the
American and British soldiers, Eisenhower's calm
invited his generals to devise a bold strategy that
took advantage of the German offensive and
opened the final march to Berlin.[2]

In business, rapidly changing markets and technologies present a continual stream of crises—and opportunities, for those brave and imaginative enough to take advantage of them. Carly Fiorina, president and CEO of Hewlett-Packard, sees opportunity for HP in a Web-enabled world. Rather than view the Web as a threat to HP, traditionally a computer hardware manufacturer, she sees the opportunity to transform HP into a company that delivers digital services through the Web, using mobile Internet appliances. Fiorina hasn't been successful—yet. But she perseveres because she believes her vision will one day soon make HP into a Web powerhouse.

Identifying and taking advantage of opportunity in a crisis takes a blend of imagination, courage, self-confidence—and faith. Both Eisenhower and King David imagined success beyond the present crisis—and found a way to defeat a superior foe. Both courageously implemented their plans in spite of overwhelming odds. Both had the self-confidence, even ambition, to pursue success. And King David believed that God would be his deliverer.

We Christian leaders believe that God is at work in our lives and organizations. Our faith gives us the self-confidence and courage we need to use our imaginations during a crisis, to uncover opportunity, and to pursue success relentlessly on behalf of those we lead.

> *God, give me the imagination and faith I need to see opportunity in the midst of crisis. Amen.*

Change Agents

The scribes and Pharisees watched him to see whether he would cure on the sabbath, so that they might find an accusation against him. Even though he knew what they were thinking, he said to the man who had the withered hand, "Come and stand here." He got up and stood there. Then Jesus said to them, "I ask you, is it lawful to do good or to do harm on the sabbath, to save life or destroy it?" After looking around at all of them, he said to him, "Stretch out your hand." He did so, and his hand was restored. But they were filled with fury and discussed with one another what they might do to Jesus.

—LUKE 6:7–11

It is an unacceptable affront to be forced to change one's mind. Individuals are what they believe, and groups are their cultures; hence to require a group to change its shared beliefs is to threaten its very existence.[3]

L eaders not only anticipate change and respond to change, they *make* change. The current business term is "change agent"; leaders are change

THE CHALLENGE OF CHANGE

agents who make change to realize visions and help organizations succeed.

The problem is that most people and their organizations are almost naturally change-resistant. Change is often perceived as a threat to be eliminated, especially when things seem to a group to be going reasonably well. A leader who is a change agent, especially a change agent in a relatively complacent organization, will almost certainly be perceived as a threat to some group within the organization. Jesus tried to change the thinking of the Pharisees and scribes about the sabbath, with the result of infuriating them and spawning plots to eliminate him.

To be effective change agents, we need a mixture of wisdom and courage, following Jesus as our guide. Jesus had the wisdom to know when people had had enough, and he backed off, retreating into a solitary place or moving on to the next town or group of people. But he was also courageous enough to push change as far as he could. It wasn't enough to lecture the Pharisees and scribes on the sabbath; he had to heal a man on the sabbath to try and get them to change their minds about the sabbath and about Jesus himself. We need to try to imitate Jesus. We need to know when our people are ready for change and so push ahead; we also need to know when they've had enough and it's time to back off. But in the end, we need to be brave enough to make necessary changes even when there is a level of resistance to us and what we are trying to do.

> *Lord, give me the wisdom and courage I
> need to be an effective change agent today.*
> *Amen.*

THE CHALLENGE OF CHANGE

The Future Is
in Your Hands

Thus says the LORD:
Keep your voice from weeping,
and your eyes from tears;
for there is a reward for your work, . . .
there is hope for your future,
says the LORD.

—JEREMIAH 31:16–17

With . . . primacy of power is also joined an awe-inspiring accountability to the future. As you look around you, you must feel not only the sense of duty done, but also you must feel anxiety lest you fall below the level of achievement. Opportunity is here now, clear and shining.[4]

During the press of the day, it's easy to overlook our responsibility to the future. As leaders, we are accountable for ensuring that our organizations continue to thrive in the future—after we're long gone. To ignore the future of our organizations or to trust that "things will just work out" is an abuse of our power. We cannot afford the luxury of resting on our executive laurels—that sense of duty well done for today. Instead, we owe it to our organizations to worry and scheme and manage how we can ensure the future success of our organizations.

Look at Jeremiah or any of the other prophets of the Bible—the leaders of their day. As wildly different from one another as they are, the prophets all share one characteristic: they view their actions, God's actions, and the actions of their people through the lens of the future. In various ways, each of them asks, *How are God's people to live and thrive in the future in such a way that will please God?* Their prophecies spell out a variety of answers to that foundational question.

As leaders today, we could do a lot worse than ask, *How is my organization to survive and thrive in such a way that will please God?* Every decision we make, every key appointment to or promotion of staff, every action we initiate, every strategy or plan we design, is part of the answer to that question. We must include a conscious consideration of the future of our organizations in all that we do today. The future success of our organizations is an opportunity that is here now—clear and shining.

> *Help me to keep one eye on the future today,*
> *O God, that my organization may*
> *continue to please you. Amen.*

Innovation:
Expect the Unexpected

> Therefore you also must be ready, for the Son of Man is coming at an unexpected hour.
>
> —MATTHEW 24:44

> A leader remains vulnerable to real surprise and to true quality. I do mean surprise—something totally unexpected. I also mean a new level of quality, one that I might not have considered before. Neither of these things is easy; really great ideas shake up organizations.[5]

We've all read about *innovation* so much and in so many different ways that it's become a word that's almost entirely devoid of meaning. Our organizations and companies, our products, our services, our work processes, our employees, and we, the leaders, are all supposed to be innovative if we are to stay competitive in a shifting, global marketplace.

But the ability to innovate—to create something entirely new and different—*is* one of the hallmarks of a leader. We ourselves may not be inventors or designers or the actual creators of a new product, service, or process, but our ability to lead means that we provide the environment where innovation happens. Leaders must remain "vulnerable to real surprise and to true quality—something totally unexpected." That's how innovation—the next new thing of great value and quality—happens in our organizations.

But beware. *Complacency* is the great enemy of innovation. Six years of mind-numbing complacency nearly ruined the company I work for. Our former leadership feared change and enjoyed coasting along complacently. Their greatest shared value was the *status quo*. Being complacent is easy. Complacency doesn't "shake things up."

Innovation, on the other hand, can surprise us and really shake up our organizations. Are we willing to be surprised? Are we willing to let things get a little crazy, maybe somewhat out of control, so that something new and valuable can be born? To gauge our comfort level with innovation, maybe we should ask ourselves how we feel about the Son of Man coming at an unexpected hour. When Jesus warned his disciples to "be ready," he was warning them against complacency, against living their lives the way they always had. Jesus was trying to tell his disciples that the coming of the Son of Man would surprise them in ways they could never imagine—and to be prepared to have their lives changed forever. Talk about shaking things up! That is what our faith does; it shakes us up and creates a place in our hearts where we are willing to be surprised by and have our lives and organizations forever changed by the always new, innovative work of God.

> *Keep me from fearing innovation, O Lord, and create in my heart more room for surprise. Amen.*

Future Leadership

> Then Jesus summoned his twelve disciples and gave them authority over unclean spirits, to cast them out, and to cure every disease and every sickness. These are the names of the twelve apostles: first, Simon, also known as Peter, and his brother Andrew; James son of Zebedee, and his brother John Philip and Bartholomew; Thomas and Matthew the tax collector; James son of Alphaeus, and Thaddaeus; Simon the Cananaean, and Judas Iscariot, the one who betrayed him.
>
> —MATTHEW 10:1–4

One of the myths of management is that good strategic planning and an appropriate vision will ensure an institution's future. I'm afraid this simply isn't enough. Only the effective selection, nurture, and assignment of senior people will secure an institution. When I ask myself about the future of an organization, this is my answer: Senior leaders *are* the future.[6]

We all know that responsible financial management of our personal assets includes creating a thoughtful estate plan. We want to take care of our families and help them survive and thrive after we are gone. Estate planning is how we ensure our families' futures.

In the business world, the equivalent of estate planning is succession planning. We want to take care of our organizations and help them survive and thrive after we are gone. Succession planning—identifying and training future leaders—is how we ensure the future of our organizations. Jesus was a master at succession planning. He knew that the success of the gospel meant identifying and training twelve key leaders to carry on after he was gone. The twelve apostles weren't perfect (Judas Iscariot needed to be replaced later), but they had promise, as well as the advantage of Jesus' personal training.

We won't be the leaders of our organizations forever. We must select those senior leaders who show promise and make a personal investment in their futures. We make a personal commitment to mentor them and give them the personal training they need to replace us. We give them real responsibility and accountability in their work, and we grant them access to any leadership training programs our organizations can offer. Our choices won't be perfect; some will cut the mustard, others won't. But the stakes are too high to leave future leadership to chance. Instead, we have faith in God at work in our organizations, and we select and train senior leaders to the best of our ability.

> *Give me the wisdom I need, O God, to find and train senior leaders who can carry on your work. Amen.*

Self-Control:
The Way of Leaders

> Like a city breached, without
> walls,
> is one who lacks self-control.
> —PROVERBS 25:28

> No man is fit to command another that cannot
> command himself.[7]

If we can't control ourselves, others will do it for us. The ability to control ourselves—to manage our appetites, our passions, our desires, our ambitions—prevents others from manipulating those passions to influence us unduly or maneuver us into serving their special interests. Lack of self-control quickly disables leaders. Without self-control, we become "like a city breached"; others rule us within our walls.

There is a vice president at our company who is famous for his charm and utter lack of self-control. He is the original "yes man." No request or demand is too trivial or thoughtless for this leader to leap immediately into action. He shows no self-control, no ability to stop and think first. He is only capable of instant response. He cannot master his desire to please. A pregnant employee once half-jokingly commented how nice it would be to have special parking places near the office reserved for expectant mothers. Instantly, our vice president got on the phone to direct corporate real estate to create maternity spaces. Coasting on charm, he is incapable of leading because he is whipsawed constantly into responding to whoever has his attention for the moment.

We are not fit to command others if we cannot command ourselves. When we command ourselves through self-control, we are able to listen to God's voice whispering among all those competing voices that would have us do their will. When we are in control, we listen to God's guidance, and we lead, thoughtfully, purposefully, effectively—faithfully.

> *With your help, O God, I am master of myself, and I will listen for your guidance and direction. Amen.*

THE CHALLENGE OF CHANGE

Creativity Brings New Life

You were taught to put away your former way of life, your old self, corrupt and deluded by its lusts, and to be renewed in the spirit of your minds, and to clothe yourselves with the new self, created according to the likeness of God in true righteousness and holiness.

—EPHESIANS 4:22–24

Real creativity, the kind that is responsible for breakthrough changes in our society, always violates the rules. That is why it is so unmanageable and that is why, in most organizations, when we say we desire creativity we really mean manageable creativity. We don't mean raw, dramatic, radical creativity that requires us to change.[8]

Writer and Christian apologist Dorothy Sayers once said that we are most like God when we create. The life of faith is a creative life, a life no less worthy than that of a brilliant artist or the most skilled craftsman. We are called to imitate God boldly in righteousness and holiness. We are called to put away our former lives and renew the spirit of our minds, clothing ourselves with new selves created in God's likeness. We engage in this daringly creative act to bring about new life not once, but continuously, constantly, endlessly—so wild, so compelling is our pursuit of God.

Our leadership should be equally creative, equally daring. As leaders, we are called to bring new life to our organizations—constantly and with great boldness. We are called to "real creativity"—the kind that can change our world, the kind that always "violates the rules." This means we are willing to live with a certain amount of wildness in our organizations, a creative kind of chaos that leads to real change, real transformation. We give up our leaderly desire to control, to manage. We encourage and reward the best, the brightest, the most creative among us. And we trust that God is working through our organizations to create new life.

Our pursuit of renewal, of transformation, our pursuit of God, is relentless and somewhat messy—the way all new life gets born.

> *Help me, O God, to bring new life, your life, to my organization. Amen.*

Teams Required

> Let us hold fast to the confession of our hope without wavering, for he who has promised is faithful. And let us consider how to provoke one another to love and good deeds, not neglecting to meet together, as is the habit of some, but encouraging one another, and all the more as you see the Day approaching.
>
> —HEBREWS 10:24–25

Finally, and most important, a leader needs a TEAM. Andrew Carnegie once said that he wanted, for his epitaph, the following words: "Here lies a man who was wise enough to bring into his service men who know more than he." The point is, you need to be able to surround yourself with bright, competent people, people who can really run this or that aspect of the business.[9]

A "Lone-Ranger Christian" is an oxymoron. No one can live a life of faith alone. We Christians need each other to keeping hoping, believing, loving, and doing good until Christ returns. It is simply impossible to be an active, practicing Christian alone on a mountaintop. Even the solitary desert monastics of the third century were accountable to other monks and nuns. We need the encouragement and accountability of a faithful team, a community of believers to keep us spiritually honest and alive.

So, too, a "Lone-Ranger leader" is an oxymoron. No leader can have all the answers for his or her organization. The world is too fluid, the marketplace too complex, technology too sophisticated for one person to "know it all." We leaders need teams staffed with "bright, competent people," experts and specialists, good managers, administrators and other leaders, who together can successfully run our businesses.

There's a definite downside to being a Lone-Ranger Christian or leader: it isn't any fun. The stimulation and challenge that comes from interacting daily with bright, competent people is a kick; they keep us thinking, they keep us learning, they keep us moving, and they make us look good. And a big part of why we get up in the morning and go to work—or to church—is to be with people we genuinely enjoy and care about. Our leadership teams, like our churches, are another kind of family for us. A good leadership team makes our work worth doing.

> *Thank you, O Lord, for my leadership team, my community here at work. Amen.*

Burning Platforms Are No Way to Run a Business

We have this hope, a sure and steadfast anchor of the soul, a hope that enters the inner shrine behind the curtain, where Jesus, a forerunner on our behalf, has entered . . .

—HEBREWS 6:19–20

Leaders everywhere seek to create "burning platforms" in order to focus the attention of followers. Almost all leaders know that there is less resistance to change in a time of crisis and, by extension, that crises legitimate asking their followers to bear pain. . . . Still, leaders can't play the crisis card repeatedly. In real life, everyone knows that either the fire gets put out or the platform will burn down. . . . Smart leaders use the threat of crisis sparingly and briefly, and then turn anxiety into energy by creating hope. . . . People who are building for a better future have almost limitless resources of energy. What you have to remember is this: *anxiety breeds exhaustion; hope creates energy.*[10]

"Burning platforms" are dangerous things. The pressure of doing business these days is hyper-intense; change never lets up and the competition is excruciating. It can be tempting and very easy to create a crisis, a burning platform, where one doesn't really exist just to move our organizations faster, farther. Even in situations where our organizations really do face a crisis and the platform really is on fire, constructively managing the crisis is extremely difficult. In attempting to manage our company's financial crisis, our CEO has lit the burning platform and then let it burn out so many times that he's become like the boy who cried wolf; employees joke darkly about cinders and smoke and ashes. The result is an employee population exhausted from all the fire drills with no resolution to the crisis, and no vision of what the company will be when the financial crisis has passed.

Instead of creating crises, God calls us to create hope. Hope is "a sure and steadfast anchor of the soul" that enables our organizations to weather any crisis, to respond quickly and definitively to any burning platform. Our Christian faith offers us as leaders a natural source of hope because we can see that our future with God in Christ is a loving one, full of mercy and grace. We can create hope for our organizations by giving them robust visions for the future—visions that show clearly what our organizations will look like and the contributions they will make to the world. During times of genuine crisis, with flames licking at our feet, such visions provide energy for our organizations to cope constructively, quickly, and decisively with the crisis.

> *Instead of crying wolf, Lord, I will create a vision for my people that will be their anchor. Amen.*

Commitment to Discipline

As you therefore have received Christ Jesus the Lord,
continue to live your lives in him, rooted and built up in
him and established in the faith, just as you were taught,
abounding in thanksgiving.

—COLOSSIANS 2:6–7

People can make lasting changes in themselves
only through a commitment to a continuing discipline. For example, crash diets don't work, but a
permanent modification of one's eating habits does.
Visits to spas don't work (after they're over), but
the daily practice of exercising, stretching, or
weight lifting does. The same is true in management. Lasting change comes only from the adop-
tion of sound management principles that are
practiced on a continuing basis. There are no quick
fixes.[11]

A friend of mine at work is near retirement after
twenty-four years of service to the company.
One day, I asked him to describe the management
changes he's seen at the company during his
career. He immediately rattled off more than a
dozen management fads company leaders have
employed over the years. He even pulled out of a

file drawer several tchotchkes given to employees to encourage them in the use of these popular management principles. I asked whether any of them worked. "Naw," he replied. "Executives would make speeches and hold big meetings for a few months; they'd give us these gifts with slogans printed on them. Then they'd forget about it, until the next fad came along."

Like many companies, our company is perpetually in search of the management principle that will be the golden fleece, the holy grail—one that will solve all its problems quickly and painlessly. It's a shame it doesn't exist. The truth is, almost any sound set of management principles will work—if used consistently as a "continuing discipline." Among leaders, it takes a commitment to discipline within ourselves to exercise better management over the long haul so that our organizations can experience lasting success.

The secret to practicing any continuing discipline is gratitude. The Letter to the Colossians underscores living a disciplined life in Christ by "abounding in thanksgiving." Beating up ourselves or, heaven help us, our staff and customers, is *not* discipline, and it never works in the long term. But if we are to be disciplined leaders consistently practicing a sound set of management principles, gratitude to God for the opportunities and challenges we see in our organizations perpetually recharges us and refreshes our commitment to do the right things consistently over time. For when we are grateful, it is hard to lose heart too early. When we are grateful, that spirit of gratitude radiates from us out among our staff members and constituents and energizes them. When we are grateful, God is very near, strengthening us and our resolve, giving us what we need to lead well.

> *Thank you, O God, for the discipline you give me to lead my organization for the long haul. Amen.*

Reflections
on God,
Life, and
Leadership

The Value of Meditation

> Happy are those who do not follow the advice of the
>   wicked,
> or take the path that sinners tread,
> or sit in the seat of scoffers;
> but their delight is in the law of the Lord
> and on his law they meditate day and night.
>
> —PSALM 1:1–2

> Values are standards or principles that guide your
> actions and beliefs. They define what is good and
> worthwhile for you. Much has been said and writ-
> ten about values in relation to leadership. . . . Being
> aware of your personal values strengthens you as a
> leader and helps you get the most personal reward
> from your leadership work.[1]

Whether we lead churches or Fortune 500
companies or community-based nonprof-
its, we remain *Christian* leaders. Our employees or
constituents may or may not know of our personal
faith. But in all that we do, our faith informs and
guides our leadership. As Christian leaders, our
beliefs influence and direct our actions. It's critical, therefore, to refresh ourselves at the well of
our faith, to keep deeply in touch with our God.

The ancient spiritual practice of meditation can serve us greatly. Meditation can keep us in touch with our values and beliefs, the wellspring of our leadership. The purpose of meditation is *not* to gather information. To meditate on God's law or the Bible is to *experience* God through the words we read, memorize, and know. Meditation on God and God's law requires that we practice something that most leaders aren't very good at—stillness. As leaders, we are rewarded for doing—for strategizing, for acting, for directing, for calling the shots. In meditation, we give up being in charge for a while—we quiet our minds and hearts. We sit still for a change, and wait and listen quietly for God's voice.

Try this. Set aside fifteen minutes a day for a week. Spend the first five minutes reading a favorite Bible verse. Spend the next five minutes praying, letting the Bible verse direct your prayers. Spend the remaining time sitting still, in silence, simply listening for God's word to you. Close by offering a prayer of thanks. And then go about your business—only this time more in touch with your values and beliefs as a Christian leader.

O God, let me experience you and your guidance in my leadership. Amen.

Regaining Balance

Rejoice in the Lord always; again I will say, Rejoice. Let your gentleness be known to everyone. The Lord is near. Do not worry about anything, but in everything by prayer and supplication let your requests be made known to God. And the peace of God, which surpasses all understanding, will guard your hearts and your minds in Christ Jesus.

—PHILIPPIANS 4:4–7

By contrast, when your life is focused and balanced, you see ways to achieve your ends, and energy can flow. Thus your effectiveness as a leader depends in part on your ability to balance or integrate your career and family involvements, your community and social lives, the pursuit of learning, and whatever else you choose to do in life. Each part of life makes legitimate demands; each offers important nourishment; your actions in each affect what you can do in the others. Balance lets you lead with full heart and soul. Effective use of your whole self allows you to go beyond "techniques" of leadership.[2]

Joy is the hallmark of a balanced life. There is a lightness of being, the peace of God, that comes from a life well lived. And joy is the result.

By contrast, worry is the hallmark of a life out of balance. Too much work with too little time for family, community, or personal pursuits produces stress and anxiety. There are prolonged absences of joy or periods of peace. A lopsided life thrown out of kilter by too much work clouds our vision with anxiety. Eventually, constant stress pressures us into making mistakes and becoming less effective in our work overall. As leaders, we have a responsibility to our organizations to lead balanced lives in touch with the God who is the source of our joy.

There is a simplicity to living a life that balances career with other personal pursuits. It is the desire to hear God speaking to us through *all* the parts of our lives. That means showing up for all the parts of our lives, whether volunteering at the local soup kitchen, taking the kids to the ball game, going out to dinner with our spouses, or spending the afternoon with a really good book. St. Paul puts it another way: the Lord is near in everything you do—so there's no need to worry; just be with God in all the parts of your life; and God will give you peace and joy.

Show me where I need to balance my life today, O God, that I may know your joy, your peace. Amen.

Prayer in Chaos

> What shall I do then? I will pray with the spirit, but I will pray with the mind also; I will sing praise with the spirit, but I will sing praise with the mind also.
>
> —1 CORINTHIANS 14:15

How can the manifestly un-Christ-like CEO of a publicly held corporation overcome resistance to change when the CEO's power is constrained by the diverse and conflicting interests of investors, board members, union chiefs, environmentalists, government regulators, and careerist managers— all intent on marching to the beat of their own drummers? Indeed, how can any leader effectively transform an organization in the midst of competitive, technological, social, and political chaos?[3]

Whether a CEO of a large company, a minister of a small congregation, or a supervisor with a dozen direct reports, part of our job as leaders is to manage chaos. Our ability to lead is definitely affected by conflicting interests, over which we have only some or no control, inside and outside of our organizations. On any given day, it can seem like we're barely controlling the chaos—and on some days chaos seems to win. What's a leader to do then?

Pray. For leaders of faith prayer keeps us in constant contact with God, who is Lord even over chaos. Prayer keeps us anchored in our unchanging God when all around us is a continual whirl.

Paul writes about two kinds of prayer: prayer of the spirit—a more spontaneous prayer from the gut, like "God, help me!" and prayer of the mind—a more thoughtful, reasoned, and reflective kind of prayer. In addition to praying with the spirit throughout the day, as responsible leaders we've got to set aside time for prayer of the mind, a time in which we seek God's guidance on the specific issues, conflicting interests, and obstacles confronting us. Prayer of the mind *thoughtfully examines our role* in these issues, humbly *offers* them to God, *asks* for God's guidance, and *listens* for God's direction. Prayer of the mind won't make the chaos go away, but when we pray thoughtfully, God will give us the guidance we need to lead our organizations through another day.

Lord, hear the prayer of my mind, and let me hear you guiding me. Amen.

Inspiration

> The spirit of God has made me,
> and the breath of the
> Almighty gives me life.
>
> —Job 33:4

Leadership energizes. Leadership breathes life into an enterprise, without which nothing truly new can emerge. The word *inspire*, long associated with leadership, derives from the Latin *inspirare*, literally "to breathe life into."[4]

It almost goes without saying that leaders must be able to inspire others. We can tell stories, guide and direct, make partnerships and alliances, plan and strategize—but the sizzle, the energy, the *life* that infuses all of our efforts is inspiration. Inspiration is what makes our employees, customers, and constituents proud of and loyal to our organizations. But where do leaders get inspiration?

From two sources. First, as leaders we must have our own heroes, those people whose leadership ability inspires us. For me, it's Carly Fiorina of Hewlett-Packard Company (HP). She's one of the very few women CEOs of an international company, which is inspiration enough. But she's also smart (she got her bachelor's degree in medieval history and philosophy from Stanford, as well as an M.B.A. and an M.S. from MIT) and very courageous. Her vision to reinvent HP—to bring the Internet to customers when and where they want it—is broad and gutsy. And she has the bravery to stand by her vision when the going gets tough.

The other source of inspiration comes from God's people. We refresh ourselves constantly by reading how God has inspired the leaders and people of the Bible. And we look for inspiration from other leaders of faith. When I was very new to the faith, I found inspiration in the Rev. Earl Palmer, former pastor of First Presbyterian Church of Berkeley. He dispelled my stereotype of Christian faith—that of a highly sentimental, thoughtless, primitive belief system. Through his sermons, Palmer showed me that faith can stand up to the rigors of intellectual discourse, and that faith speaks directly to the complex, contemporary issues that confront each of us daily.

God still breathes over, and inspires, creation. When we open ourselves to be inspired by God and leaders in business and in faith, we can breathe that same life into our organizations.

Lord, inspire me. And help me to inspire others in my organization today. Amen.

Source of Our Power

Of this gospel I have become a servant according to
the gift of God's grace that was given me by the working
of his power.

—Ephesians 3:7

Preside in order to promote the good of those
whom you govern. . . . Provide rather than dominate. I fear for you, for there is no poison more
dangerous . . ., nor sword more deadly, than the
lust to dominate.[5]

At some time or other, all of us have experienced leaders possessed of the "lust to dominate." And what a miserable experience that was!
We, of course, would never actively dominate our
organizations. But the temptation to misuse our
power is an insidious poison; it can sit long upon
the shelf, waiting to be drunk during a time when
the going gets tough and our organizations are
threatened by overwhelming chaos. It is then that
we are in the most danger of dominating our
organizations; it is, we tell ourselves, *for their
own good.*

To promote the good of our organizations, to provide for and support them rather than dominate them during times of trial, we need to experience the source of our power: God's grace. We lead our organizations by God's grace alone. Our leadership is a gift from God. It is God who put us there—and it is God who can remove us. And God put us in these leadership positions, not to promote our own personal agendas, but to serve God and to exercise God's power, which is always power expressed in love and mercy. We are servant leaders of a powerful, graceful, and provident God. The lust to dominate evaporates when we open our hearts daily, with thanksgiving and humility, to God's unending grace.

> *Lord, I open my heart to your grace, that I may better serve you in my organization. Amen.*

Growing Through
Self-Examination

Examine yourselves to see whether you are living in the faith. Test yourselves. Do you not realize that Jesus Christ is in you?—unless, indeed, you fail to meet the test!

—2 CORINTHIANS 13:5

Firing people is always difficult. It's the moment of truth for a business leader. You never face the problem of firing somebody without truthfully, honestly examining the question of how much you yourself contributed to the situation. Are you firing him because of . . . general economic conditions? If so, then it isn't his fault, it's yours. You're supposed to run the company so that it would be strong enough to weather bad economic conditions. . . . You may be firing him because he's done a poor job. . . . Did he do a bad job because he was not helped? He was entitled to help. . . . Perhaps a man was failing because he inherited a tough problem that no one else can solve; or he is caught in a situation completely beyond his control. . . . It was you who put him in deep water over his head.[6]

It is impossible to grow and develop as a leader unless we're willing to regularly examine our motives, decisions, and actions. Harold Geneen, former CEO of ITT, writes that "the moment of truth" for leaders comes when we must fire employees. Firing someone is such a grave action with such serious consequences that we must examine ourselves as leaders to learn how we may have unwittingly or knowingly contributed to an employee's failure—and learn from the experience and change our behaviors accordingly.

Too often these days, many Protestant churches rush to comfort parishioners, skipping over any deeply reflective, meaningful search of self for sin, and going straight to repentance and grace. Such churches do a serious disservice to Christians. By not helping provide a framework for serious self-examination, churches deny Christians the opportunity to grow and change deeply, which is the whole experience of genuine repentance. This means it's often up to individual Christians to examine their hearts and souls under the eye of God.

As Christian leaders, we can examine our hearts and souls and minds—and experience repentance and forgiveness, and grow and change. We can take advantage of those moments of truth in our leadership and ask ourselves questions such as these:

- How did I contribute to this situation?
- What were my motives behind my action?
- Did I fail to think through my decision? If so, what did I overlook?

- Who is paying the consequences of my decision/action?
- How can I make amends or correct the situation?

Then we take our answers, take any sin we find in them to God, and ask God's forgiveness and the courage to change.

> *O God, give me the courage to examine my own heart and soul that I may be touched and changed by your unflinching mercy.*
> *Amen.*

Remember Who You Are
and Whom You Represent

> Paul, a servant of Jesus Christ, called to be an apostle, set
> apart for the gospel of God.
>
> —ROMANS 1:1

> In all of his works, Greenleaf discusses the need for
> a new kind of leadership model, a model that puts
> serving others—including employees, customers
> and community—as the number one priority. Ser-
> vant-leadership emphasizes increased service to
> others, a holistic approach to work, promoting a
> sense of community, and the sharing of power in
> decision making. Who is a servant-leader? . . . The
> servant-leader is one who is a servant first.[7]

Many years ago, I worked for a publisher of
religious books. A group of us were attending a sales meeting in New York. One evening, we
were leaving our hotel to get some supper. On his
way to another appointment, the publisher of the
company passed us on the sidewalk and said,
"Remember who you are and whom you represent." He was only half joking. Our publisher was
reminding us to behave ourselves in the Big Apple
because how we behaved reflected on the company.

At the very outset of his letter to the Romans, the apostle Paul sets the record straight: he is first and foremost a servant of Jesus Christ. Everything Paul writes flows from the understanding of his role as a servant. God calls each of us to be servants to our organizations. Like Paul, we are servant-leaders, set apart for the gospel of God and God's community. How well we serve our organizations reflects on *who* we are—Christians in the service of our God. Our behavior as servant-leaders reflects on *whom* we represent—our organizations.

And servant-leadership is good business. Our employees, customers, vendors, analysts, bankers, industries, and communities frequently judge our organizations by how we behave in our quest for success. As leaders, we have the power to shape others' perceptions of our organizations—for better or worse. Promoting a holistic approach to work, building a sense of community, and sharing power in decision making tells the world who we are and whom we represent. When we genuinely seek to serve our organizations first, putting their success above ours, our servant-leadership reflects well on our organizations—and God.

> *Give me the skills I need to be a servant-leader, O God, that the world may know who I am and whom I represent. Amen.*

We Are Symbols

But the people refused to listen to the voice of Samuel;
they said, "No! but we are determined to have a king over
us, so that we also may be like other nations, and that our
king may govern us and go out before us and fight our
battles." When Samuel had heard all the words of the
people, he repeated them in the ears of the Lord. The
Lord said to Samuel, "Listen to their voice and set a king
over them."

—1 SAMUEL 8:19–22

Leaders are inevitably symbols. Workers singled
out to be supervisors discover that they are set
apart from their old comrades in subtle ways. They
try to keep the old camaraderie but things have
changed. They are now symbols of management.
Sergeants symbolize the chain of command. Parish
religious leaders symbolize their churches. . . . One
function that cannot be delegated is that of serving
as symbol. That the leader as a symbol is a fact, not
a matter of choice. The task is to take appropriate
account of that reality and use it well in the service
of the group's goals.[8]

That "leaders are inevitably symbols" is a con-
cept as old as humanity. When Israel, jealous
of other nations, demanded a king to govern them

and fight their battles, it was a symbolic rejection of God's leadership. No longer would God govern them through a series of judges; no longer would God deliver them from their enemies. Only a king would do—a king who would act symbolically in God's place. And the subsequent stories of Israel and her kings and her God were both glorious and stormy.

Like it or not, we leaders are not ourselves; rather, we are powerful symbols. We are representatives of our corporations, of our organizations' collective values and dreams, of our municipalities or our country—and sometimes even of God. In order to be effective symbols for our organizations, we must be conscious of the fact that we *are* symbols for our organizations. And we must be honest about how we feel about what (or whom) we represent. We must accept the fact that we are symbols and be relatively comfortable with that fact. We are *not* substitutes for God, but we do represent something much, much bigger than ourselves.

The symbols of our leadership are powerful tools. When we put on that robe, sit in the spacious corner office with a view, or stand behind a lectern before hundreds, we have tremendous power to use these symbols of our leadership to serve our groups' goals. With humility under the eye of God and full consciousness of what we symbolize, we can use the trappings of our offices

to inspire, motivate, command, persuade, and
lead—all in order to make our groups' dreams a
reality.

> *I am more than I appear to be, O God.*
> *Help me to be wise in how I use the symbols*
> *of my leadership. Amen.*

The Lightness of Being

[Jesus] said to his disciples, "Therefore I tell you, do not worry about your life, what you will eat, or about your body, what you will wear. For life is more than food and the body more than clothing."

—LUKE 12:22

When trying to effect change of any significance, it is inevitable that some extremely stressful, serious barriers will be encountered. Even projects that at first glance appear very simple and sensible may present difficulties that are impossible to foresee. . . . Humor can serve as a valuable asset to release the tension and stress created in such situations.[9]

A friend of mine leads one of the business units at our company. She once told me, "I love my work, and I feel extremely responsible and accountable for what me and my staff produce. But life is too short to get ulcers over it. I do the very best I can, and I try to make work fun and meaningful for everybody. After that I sort of let go." My friend intuitively knows that "life is more than food and the body more than clothing." A constant diet of worry and stress doesn't get the job done; hard work with as much fun and humor mixed in as possible does the job.

Our organizations are extremely important to us. The changes our organizations face will have a critical impact on whether they survive or thrive. We take very seriously our leadership roles and responsibilities. As Christian leaders, we know that ultimately our organizations rest in God's hands. God has placed us in our organizations to guide them to the best of our abilities; the rest belongs to God. While taking our work seriously, we also take it lightly. We can enjoy our work—and make work enjoyable for others—because we know there's more to life than work.

Holding our organizations lightly also has a physical benefit. Enjoying our work and having a sense of humor about it helps to ease worry and stress, and that will help prevent burn-out or other serious health problems. God didn't build us to be anxiety machines; God built us to enjoy each other and all of God's creation.

O God, help me to lighten up today. Amen.

Beliefs Make Leaders

I came that they may have life, and have it abundantly.

—JOHN 10:10

If people are machines, seeking to control us makes sense. But if we live with the same forces intrinsic to all other life, then seeking to impose control through rigid structures is suicide. If we believe that there is no order to human activity except that imposed by the leader, that there is no self-regulation except that dictated by policies, if we believe that responsible leaders must have their hands into everything, controlling every decision, person, and moment, then we cannot hope for anything except what we already have—a treadmill of frantic efforts that end up destroying our individual and collective vitality.[10]

Ultimately, what we believe about our organizations, and the people in them, determines what kind of leaders we are. An executive in our financially troubled company recently remarked, "I don't care about employees; they'll do what we tell 'em." His statement indicates that he believes *he* is the organization and that employees are automatons. No wonder this leader "leads" by "command and control." In contrast, another executive at our company made the following statement: "We'll never get out of the mess we're in if we don't figure out ways to develop engaged, informed employees who are excited about working here every day." This leader clearly believes that employees are human beings who *are* the company. No wonder this leader includes employees in critical decision making and is enthusiastic about his staff. Who would you rather work hard for? Who would you rather be?

Jesus came that we might have life, and have it abundantly—in this world and in the next. Jesus did not treat people as organic machines passively waiting to do his bidding; he treated them as human beings with minds, hearts, souls, and bodies—people who desperately wanted an abundant life. As Christian leaders, we cannot believe in mechanical organizations that consist of employee-cogs to make them run. Instead, because of the Christ we follow, we believe that our organizations are living things composed of living human beings who deserve to be treated with respect and dignity. We believe that our employees are people who desire and deserve an abundant life—not only in heaven, but in this life—in their families, their communities, and their workplaces. And that belief will determine the kinds of leaders we will be.

> *Give me the courage, O Lord, to examine what I really believe about the people in my organization. Amen.*

Seeing Is Believing

There were two blind men sitting by the roadside. When they heard that Jesus was passing by, they shouted, "Lord, have mercy on us, Son of David!" Jesus stood still and called them, saying, "What do you want me to do for you?" They said to him, "Lord, let our eyes be opened." Moved with compassion, Jesus touched their eyes. Immediately they regained their sight and followed him.

—MATTHEW 20:30–34

It is common to speak of self-fulfilling prophecies and the impact these have on people's behavior. If a manager is told that a new trainee is particularly gifted, that manager will see genius emerging from the trainee's mouth. . . . But if the manager is told that his or her new hire is a bit slow on the uptake, the manager will interpret a brilliant idea as a sure sign of sloppy thinking. . . . We have already decided that [employees who've been "anointed"] will succeed, so we continually observe them with the expectation that they will confirm our beliefs. Others in organizations go unobserved, forever invisible, bundles of potential that no one bothers to look at . . . and [they] are thereafter locked into jobs that provide them with no opportunity to display new potential.[11]

I remember Mrs. Sylvester, my fourth-grade teacher. She thought I could do anything, and told me so again and again. I rose to match her expectations of me. Under her leadership I became someone I'd never been before: the best student in the class. I remember once being assigned to a boss who didn't want me on his team. He had a pretty low opinion of my skills and abilities, and he told me so again and again. My performance sunk to his level of expectations of me. While working for this boss, I became someone I'd never been before: a professional failure.

At one time or another, we've all experienced the power of someone else's "self-fulfilling prophecy." It's important to remember that power as we lead our organizations. Because what we see is all too often exactly what we'll get. Rather than indulge in our prophetic abilities with regard to individuals in our organizations, it's far better to see people with Jesus' eyes. Even Jesus didn't make any assumptions about the two blind men he met on the roadside. He didn't assume that because they were blind they wanted to be healed, so he asked what it was they wanted from him. I think that when Jesus heard that the men wanted their eyes to be opened, Jesus saw something of himself, something of his humanity, his divinity, in those blind men—and he was deeply moved. When we try to see the people who work for us as Jesus sees them, we often see Jesus in them. This doesn't mean that simply seeing others through Jesus' eyes will mean that nobody ever gets fired or gets into trouble or is in the wrong job. But it does mean that when we stop for a minute and ask Jesus to open our eyes, just maybe we'll get a clearer, more real picture of the person in front of us—and treat that person with a deeply felt compassion.

> *Let me see the people in my organization with your eyes, O Lord. Amen.*

Insight

Lay aside immaturity, and live,
and walk in the way of insight.

—PROVERBS 9:6

I am using *feeling* for a mode of knowing that is not
irrational but at the same time may not meet the
strictest criteria of logic and completeness. The
process by which we get clear on something, by
which we "see what needs to be done," by which
we develop a sense of pacing and timing. . . . In
very complex, very fast-moving situations, we
depend on these abilities. We don't know much
about exactly how they can be developed and
strengthened, but I certainly think any management program is deficient that does not recognize
the reality of these abilities in leadership and management.[12]

There is a moment for athletes, musicians, and
mystics when it all comes together—body,
mind, and heart all work together seamlessly,
unconsciously, to do what they do best. It's that
"sweet spot" in which one is totally unaware of
technique—one only knows movement, music,
communion.

Leaders know that "sweet spot," too. It's a feeling, but it's more than a feeling; it's that flash of insight, of knowing, of feeling just what to do and when to do it. That burst of insight seems to come unbidden yet often during those "very complex, very fast-moving situations" when we need it the most. Over the years, with practice and experience, we've come to depend on "the way of insight." And after the current situation or crisis has passed or been resolved, we know that relying on insight is *why* we're leaders in the first place; we know that it's the only way to live.

As leaders of faith, we know that the author of insight is God. We know that walking the way of insight is a way of walking in faith. It's how God talks to us; it's how we talk to God.

> *For the gift of insight, O God, I give you thanks and praise. Amen.*

Pray Without Ceasing

Rejoice always, pray without ceasing, give thanks in all circumstances; for this is the will of God in Christ Jesus for you.

—1 THESSALONIANS 5:16–18

Yes, I think prayer is hard because of the shift it requires within us. This is perhaps the deepest mode of leadership we can speak of—the decision by a leader to turn toward the spirit in self and in others and begin to try to experience it more fully in prayer. Will this result in greater profits? More efficient attainment of objectives? . . . We have no way of knowing. It *will* result in more spiritually grounded action, whatever that turns out to be.[13]

Prayer is more than something we leaders do on our knees. Leadership is a kind of prayer. It is prayer that does not cease. Every action we take as leaders can be a prayer. Because every action we take tells God something important about us. How we coach a member of our team tells God how we really feel about the community God calls us to. How we discipline or dismiss an employee tells God about how much mercy and gentleness lives in our hearts. How we communicate with our organizations tells God about how well we love the truth. How much, or how little, we share power with our key staff members tells God how much we trust God with our organizations. And so on. And in every action we take as leaders, God is telling us something important about God in our lives. When we listen to our organizations, when we hear and accept constructive feedback, we hear God helping us to be better leaders. When we lavish care on developing and communicating our visions for our organizations, we hear God working through us. When we make good, solid decisions that help our organizations take meaningful action in the world, we hear God affirming our call to leadership.

Prayer is hard because it does require a shift in us—a shift in our interior perception that sees the holy in the ordinary. Try this for a few days: make every act you do as a leader a prayer. At the end of each day, reflect on what your actions, your prayers, told God. And reflect on what you heard God telling you through your actions.

> *Let every act I take today, O God, be a prayer to you. Amen.*

The Price of Justice

It is not right to be partial to the guilty,
or to subvert the innocent in judgment.

—PROVERBS 18:5

Today's figurative equivalent of a [public] hanging
is, of course, the firing or dismissal of managers
who violate important organizational norms. When
corporate leaders sack supervisors who have abused
workers, when they dismiss managers who have
embezzled or bribed, and when they force resigna-
tions of key executives whose behavior blatantly
belies stated organizational values, they send powerful messages throughout employee ranks. . . .
Cowardly leaders fire offenders who are weak and
insignificant; courageous leaders fire high-profile,
powerful—and even productive—individuals who
brazenly and defiantly choose to foul the organization's well.[14]

The first church in which I served as an assistant minister was led by a senior pastor, who
had a long history of inappropriate sexual relationships with women in a number of different
congregations. Rather than discipline this man, the
Presbyterian church quietly arranged for him to

find work at a different church each time a complaint was made. I don't know what happened to the women involved. I learned of this pastor's history only after I left the ministry. I also learned that the Presbyterian church wasn't the only church to cover up their leaders' moral indiscretions. Organizations do it all the time. Sometimes the price of justice is getting rid of our friends.

We leaders earn our pay doing the right thing by our organizations and all of their constituents. When our employees or our managers "brazenly and defiantly choose to foul the organization's well," we must have the courage to discipline offenders publicly. Failure to do so reflects personal, moral, and spiritual failure on our own part. As hard as publicly disciplining or dismissing someone is, the Bible is clear: "It is not right to be partial to the guilty, or to subvert the innocent in judgment." When we act justly and make an example of employees who indulge in egregious behavior, we send a message to our employees and constituents that we lead honorable organizations worthy of the trust our employees, customers, and vendors place in us. When we refuse to tolerate those who violate our organizations' values, we show God that we are worthy of God's faith in us.

> *Hard though it sometimes is, Lord, I know you will help me do the right thing. Amen.*

Questions Are More Important Than Answers

> What then are we to say about these things? If God is for us, who is against us? He who did not withhold his own Son, but gave him up for all of us, will he not with him also give us everything else? Who will bring any charge against God's elect? It is God who justifies. Who is to condemn? It is Christ Jesus, who died, yes, who was raised, who is at the right hand of God, who indeed intercedes for us. Who will separate us from the love of Christ? Will hardship, or distress, or persecution, or famine, or nakedness, or peril or sword?
>
> —ROMANS 8:31–35

As Harvard's Ronald Heifetz explains, "Leaders do not need to know all the answers. They do need to know the right questions."[15]

When I worked for a publishing house, representatives from the editorial and marketing departments met weekly to decide which books we would publish and which ones we would decline. Our publisher chaired the meetings, and it was he who ultimately decided the books we would publish. The publisher was a genuinely brilliant leader in many ways. He was a master of guiding discussion; he would steer the discussion of various book projects by asking pointed, thoughtful questions of people around the table. His questions were carefully designed to get people to think about what they were really saying, what they really meant to do. His questions stirred debate and helped the group get to the heart of the matter.

Paul was a leader who knew the power of questions to get to the heart of a matter. His series of questions in Romans compel us to stop thinking of God as some detached, all-powerful being. Paul's questions build powerfully on each other to reveal the truth that God is our faithful, passionate lover, who steadfastly takes our side and refuses to be separated from us. Paul's questions quicken our minds, stir our souls, and put fire in our hearts.

We don't need to know all the answers. We do need to know the right questions. We need to ask those questions that will lead our organizations to discover who it is they need to be, what it is they need to do, and how they are going to do it. We need to ask those questions that will inspire, motivate, and empower people to be and do their best in a complex, competitive world. We need to ask those questions that will set hearts on fire.

> *Lord, help me to ask those questions that will help my organization learn who they are and what they need to do. Amen.*

God Chooses

The Lord said, "Rise and anoint him; for this is the one."
Then Samuel took the horn of oil, and anointed him in
the presence of his brothers; and the spirit of the Lord
came mightily upon David from that day forward.

—1 SAMUEL 16:12–13

[Ulysses S. Grant] was a good subaltern, a poor
farmer, a worse tanner, a worthless trafficker [mer-
chant]. Without civil experience, literary gifts, too
diffident to be ambitious, too modest to put himself forward, too honest to be a politician, he was of
all men the least likely to attain eminence, and
absolutely unfitted, apparently, for preeminence;
yet God's providence selected him. . . . Ordained
was Grant with the ointment of war—black and
sulphurous.[16]

On September 10, 2001, Rudolf Giuliani was
a somewhat better-than-average politician
and the mayor of New York. On September 11, he
became a leader. The crisis of the terrorist attacks
on the World Trade Center in Manhattan made
Giuliani a leader. He rose to the occasion—spending long hours with police and firefighters at
Ground Zero as they tried to rescue victims,

speaking eloquent words to the world that moved all of us deeply. Giuliani let his human nature overcome his political nature, thereby becoming a leader who will be remembered throughout history.

We can work hard at leading and gain experience for years and years, but we may never get the chance to really lead. At the end of the day, we don't get to choose to be leaders; only God chooses. David was a nobody from Bethlehem, the runt of Jesse's litter, until God chose him through Samuel as King Saul's successor. Only God chooses, God anoints those leaders who will go down in the history of their organizations, their communities, their countries, the world.

Often, God chooses leaders through crisis. Ulysses S. Grant, a failure in peace, was made a leader in the crucible of war. It's not by accident that we get to be "at the right place at the right time"; only God puts us in the right place at the right time. We can only prepare, commit to do beyond our best, and pray that, should a crisis come, we, too, can rise by the power of God, to the occasion.

> *I am ready, O God, to be used by you however you choose. Amen.*

Conflict Is Good

Beloved, let us love one another, because love is from God; everyone who loves is born of God and knows God.

—1 JOHN 4:7

Effective decision-makers deliberately . . . create dissension and disagreement, rather than consensus. Decisions of the kind the executive has to make are not made well by acclamation. They are made well only if based on the clash of conflicting views, the dialogue between different points of view, the choice between different judgments. The first rule in decision-making is that one does not make a decision unless there is disagreement.[17]

Many Christians suffer from the wrongheaded notion that conflict is bad. The assumption is that conflict means trouble—that conflict is a symptom of bad feelings and ill will. But that isn't always true. Conflict can be creative—*when the feelings and motivations behind it are based on mutual respect and trust—and love.*

Creative conflict makes good decisions. Airing conflicting views can help us leaders see more alternatives, gain new perspectives on issues, discover new avenues for action. The difference between creative and destructive conflict lies in the motivation of those taking part in the discussion.

We've all heard people begin to express an opposing view by saying, "Don't take this personally. . . ." But creative conflict *is* personal. In order for conflict to work for us as leaders and decision makers, we need to be assured of the very personal motivations behind those expressing conflicting viewpoints. To know whether their *hearts* are in the right place, we need to ask the following questions:

- Do these people want what's best for our organization?
- Do they support the guiding vision or mission of our organization?
- Do they trust and respect their colleagues and leaders to decide the right thing to do at the end of the discussion?
- Will they fully support whatever decision leadership makes based on our discussion?

Creative conflict is an act of love, a love born of God. Mutual respect and trust is the secret to healthy conflict, because "respect" and "trust" are the business expressions of "love" and respect and trust are how we love one another professionally. All true love is from God—and in our professional lives, we can look for that love expressed as personal, mutual respect, and trust as we make important decisions with our organizations.

I trust the presence of your love in mutual respect and trust among those I work most closely with, O Lord. Amen.

Notes

THE CHARACTER OF A LEADER

1. Maxwell, J. C. *The 21 Irrefutable Laws of Leadership: Follow Them and People Will Follow You.* Nashville, Tenn.: Nelson, 1998, p. 23.

2. Quinn, R. *Deep Change: Discovering the Leader Within.* San Francisco: Jossey-Bass, 1996, pp. 78–79.

3. Kouzes, J., and Posner, B. *The Leadership Challenge: How to Keep Getting Extraordinary Things Done in Organizations.* (2nd ed.) San Francisco: Jossey-Bass, 1995, p. 93.

4. Gooden, W. E. "Confidence Under Pressure." In R. Banks and K. Powell, eds., *Faith in Leadership: How Leaders Live Out Their Faith in Their Work and Why It Matters.* San Francisco: Jossey-Bass, 2000, p. 47.

5. O'Toole, J. *Leading Change: Overcoming the Ideology of Comfort and the Tyranny of Custom.* San Francisco: Jossey-Bass, 1995, p. 7.

6. Hesselbein, F., Goldsmith, M., and Somerville, I. (eds.). *Leading Beyond the Walls: How High-Performing Organizations Collaborate for Shared Success.* San Francisco: Jossey-Bass, 1999, p. 156.

7. Farson, R. *Management of the Absurd: Paradoxes in Leadership.* New York: Simon & Schuster, 1996, pp. 106 and 108.
8. Farson, 1996, p. 53.
9. Farson, 1996, pp. 126 and 128.
10. Farson, 1996, p. 152.
11. Palmer, P. J. "Leading from Within." In L. C. Spears, ed., *Insights on Leadership: Service, Stewardship, Spirit, and Servant-leadership.* New York: Wiley, 1997, p. 200.
12. Gardner, J. W. "The Cry for Leadership." In J. T. Wren, ed., *The Leader's Companion: Insights on Leadership through the Ages.* (7th ed.) New York: Free Press, 1995, pp. 5–6.
13. Covey, S. R. *Principle-Centered Leadership.* (11th ed.) New York: Summit Books, 1990, p. 107.
14. Vaill, P. B. *Spirited Leading and Learning: Process Wisdom for a New Age.* San Francisco: Jossey-Bass, 1998, p. 113.
15. O'Toole, J. *Leadership from A to Z: A Guide for the Appropriately Ambitious.* San Francisco: Jossey-Bass, 1999, p. 312.

THE LEADER'S VOCATION
1. Jinkins, M., and Jinkins, D. B. *The Character of Leadership: Political Realism and Public Virtue in Nonprofit Organizations.* San Francisco: Jossey-Bass, 1998, p. 19.
2. Wheatley, M. J. *Leadership and the New Science: Discovering Order in a Chaotic World.* (2nd ed.) San Francisco: Berrett-Koehler, 1999, p. 68.
3. Gardner, J. W. *On Leadership.* (9th paperback ed.) New York: Free Press, 1990, pp. 104–105.

QUALITIES OF EXCELLENT LEADERS

1. Hagberg, J. O. "Sharing Power as an Expression of Faith." In R. Banks and K. Powell, eds., *Faith in Leadership: How Leaders Live Out Their Faith in Their Work and Why It Matters.* San Francisco: Jossey-Bass, 2000, p. 106.

2. Lee, R. J., and King, S. N. *Discovering the Leader in You: A Guide to Realizing Your Personal Leadership Potential.* San Francisco: Jossey-Bass, 2001, p. 32.

3. Kouzes, J. M., and Posner, B. Z. *Encouraging the Heart: A Leader's Guide to Rewarding and Recognizing Others.* San Francisco: Jossey-Bass, 1999, p. 79.

4. Kouzes and Posner, 1999, p. 105.

5. "Presidential Aide Jack Valenti Recalls the Lessons Learned at the Center of Power." In W. Safire, ed., *Lend Me Your Ears: Great Speeches in History.* (2nd ed.) New York: Norton, 1997, p. 592.

6. Farson, R. *Management of the Absurd: Paradoxes in Leadership.* New York: Simon & Schuster, 1996, p. 86.

7. Farson, 1996, p. 145.

8. Kelley, R. E. "Followership in a Leadership World." In L. C. Spears, ed., *Insights on Leadership: Service, Stewardship, Spirit, and Servant-Leadership.* (5th ed.) New York: Wiley, 1998, pp. 171 and 177.

9. Frick, D. M. "Understanding Robert K. Greenleaf and Servant-Leadership." In L. C. Spears, ed., *Insights on Leadership: Service,* New York: Wiley, 1998, p. 354.

10. Gardner, J. W. *On Leadership.* (9th paperback ed.) New York: Free Press, 1990, pp. 48–49.
11. Gardner, 1990, p. 52.
12. Covey, S. R. *Principle-Centered Leadership.* (11th ed.) New York: Summit Books, 1990, p. 25.
13. Covey, 1990, p. 72.
14. O'Toole, J. *Leadership from A to Z: A Guide for the Appropriately Ambitious.* San Francisco: Jossey-Bass, 1999, p. 91.
15. O'Toole, 1999, p. 207.
16. O'Toole, 1999, p. 237.
17. Nadler, D. A., and Tushman, M. L. "Beyond the Charismatic Leader." In J. T. Wren, ed., *The Leader's Companion: Insights on Leadership Through the Ages.* (7th ed.) New York: Free Press, 1995, p. 112.

LEADING WITH GRACE

1. Gooden, W. E. "Confidence Under Pressure." In R. Banks and K. Powell, eds., *Faith in Leadership: How Leaders Live Out Their Faith in Their Work and Why It Matters.* San Francisco: Jossey-Bass, 2000, p. 50.
2. Jinkins, M., and Jinkins, D. B. *The Character of Leadership: Political Realism and Public Virtue in Nonprofit Organizations.* San Francisco: Jossey-Bass, 1998, p. 63.
3. Jinkins and Jinkins, 1998, p. 94.
4. Jinkins and Jinkins, 1998, p. 123.
5. De Pree, M. *Leading Without Power: Finding Hope in Serving Community.* San Francisco: Jossey-Bass, 1997, p. 53.

6. Kouzes, J. M., and Posner, B. Z. *Encouraging the Heart: A Leader's Guide to Rewarding and Recognizing Others.* San Francisco: Jossey-Bass, 1999, p. 62.

7. Kouzes and Posner, 1999, p. 73.

8. Kouzes and Posner, 1999, p. 77.

9. Kouzes and Posner, 1999, p. 131.

10. O'Toole, J. *Leading Change: Overcoming the Ideology of Comfort and the Tyranny of Custom.* San Francisco: Jossey-Bass, 1995, p. 250.

11. Hesselbein, F., Goldsmith, M., and Somerville, I. (eds.). *Leading Beyond the Walls: How High-Performing Organizations Collaborate for Shared Success.* San Francisco: Jossey-Bass, 1999, p. 44.

12. Hesselbein, Goldsmith, and Somerville (eds.), 1999, p. 78.

13. Merton, T. "New Seeds of Contemplation." In H. Fleiss, ed., *Essential Monastic Wisdom: Writings on the Contemplative Life.* San Francisco: Harper San Francisco, 1999, p. 98.

14. Chittister, J. "The Rule of Benedict." In H. Fleiss, ed., *Essential Monastic Wisdom: Writings on the Contemplative Life.* San Francisco: Harper San Francisco, 1999.

15. "Presidential Aide Jack Valenti Recalls the Lessons Learned at the Center of Power." In W. Safire, ed., *Lend Me Your Ears: Great Speeches in History.* (2nd ed.) New York: Norton, 1997, p. 594.

16. De Pree, M. *Leadership Jazz.* New York: Doubleday, 1992, p. 154.

17. Farson, R. *Management of the Absurd: Paradoxes in Leadership.* New York: Simon & Schuster, 1996, p. 114.

18. Farson, 1996, p. 158.
19. Greenleaf, R. K. *Servant Leadership: A Journey into the Nature of Legitimate Power and Greatness.* Mahwah, N.J.: Paulist Press, 1977, p. 19.
20. Smith, R. B. "Talent and Training for Leadership." In J. T. Wren, ed., *The Leader's Companion: Insights on Leadership Through the Ages.* (7th ed.) New York: Free Press, 1995, p. 471.
21. Drucker, P. F. *The Effective Executive.* (40th paperback ed.) New York: HarperCollins, 1985, pp. 100 and 112.
22. Matusak, L. R. *Finding Your Voice: Learning to Lead . . . Anywhere You Want to Make a Difference.* (3rd ed.) San Francisco: Jossey-Bass, 1997, p. 41.
23. Matusak, 1997, p. 41.
24. Wheatley, M. J. *Leadership and the New Science: Discovering Order in a Chaotic World.* (2nd ed.) San Francisco: Berrett-Koehler, 1999, pp. 39–40.
25. Wheatley, 1999, p. 46.
26. Drucker, P. F. *Management Challenges for the 21st Century.* (11th ed.) New York: HarperBusiness, 1999, p. 130.
27. Drucker, 1999, pp. 188–189.
28. Covey, S. R. *Principle-Centered Leadership.* (11th ed.) New York: Summit Books, 1990, pp. 157–158.
29. O'Toole, J. *Leadership from A to Z: A Guide for the Appropriately Ambitious.* San Francisco: Jossey-Bass, 1999, p. 73.
30. O'Toole, 1999, pp. 161–163.
31. O'Toole, 1999, pp. 250–251.
32. Burns, J. M. "Transactional and Transforming Leadership." In J. T. Wren, ed., *The Leader's Companion,* p. 101.

THE LEADERSHIP VISION

1. Gooden, W. E. "Confidence Under Pressure." In R. Banks and K. Powell, eds., *Faith in Leadership: How Leaders Live Out Their Faith in Their Work and Why It Matters.* San Francisco: Jossey-Bass, 2000, p. 58.

2. Lee, R. J., and King, S. N. *Discovering the Leader in You: A Guide to Realizing Your Personal Leadership Potential.* San Francisco: Jossey-Bass, 2001, p. 55.

3. Farson, R. *Management of the Absurd: Paradoxes in Leadership.* New York: Simon & Schuster, 1996, p. 28.

4. Schein, E. H. "Defining Organizational Culture." In J. T. Wren, ed., *The Leader's Companion: Insights on Leadership Through the Ages.* (7th ed.) New York: Free Press, 1995, p. 273.

5. Gardner, J. W. *On Leadership.* (9th paperback ed.) New York: Free Press, 1990, pp. 31–32.

6. O'Toole, J. *Leadership from A to Z: A Guide for the Appropriately Ambitious.* San Francisco: Jossey-Bass, 1999, pp. 254–255.

THE CHALLENGE OF CHANGE

1. d'Avila-Latourrette, V.-A. *A Monastic Year.* Dallas: Taylor, 1996, p. 100.

2. Jinkins, M., and Jinkins, D. B. *The Character of Leadership: Political Realism and Public Virtue in Nonprofit Organizations.* San Francisco: Jossey-Bass, 1998, p. 135.

3. O'Toole, J. *Leading Change: Overcoming the Ideology of Comfort and the Tyranny of Custom.* San Francisco: Jossey-Bass, 1995, pp. 257–258.

4. "Winston Churchill Warns the West of the Soviet 'Iron Curtain.'" In W. Safire, ed., *Lend Me Your Ears: Great Speeches in History.* (2nd ed.) New York: Norton, 1997, p. 866.

5. De Pree, M. *Leadership Jazz.* New York: Doubleday, 1992, p. 97.

6. De Pree, 1992, p. 209.

7. Penn, W. *No Cross, No Crown: The Original Exposition on the Cross of Jesus Christ.* Mercy Place, 2001. (*No Cross, No Crown* originally published 1669.)

8. Farson, R. *Management of the Absurd: Paradoxes in Leadership.* New York: Simon & Schuster, 1996, p. 103.

9. Smith, R. B. In J. T. Wren, ed., *The Leader's Companion: Insights on Leadership Through the Ages.* (7th ed.) New York: Free Press, 1995, pp. 469–470.

10. O'Toole, J. *Leadership from A to Z: A Guide for the Appropriately Ambitious.* San Francisco: Jossey-Bass, 1999, pp. 230–231.

11. Farson, 1996, p. 121.

REFLECTIONS ON GOD, LIFE, AND LEADERSHIP

1. Lee, R. J., and King, S. N. Discovering the Leader in You: A Guide to Realizing Your Personal Leadership Potential. San Francisco: Jossey-Bass, 2001, p. 103.

2. Lee and King, 2001, p. 148.

3. O'Toole, J. *Leading Change: Overcoming the Ideology of Comfort and the Tyranny of Custom.* San Francisco: Jossey-Bass, 1995, pp. 11–12.

4. Hesselbein, F., Goldsmith, M., and Somerville, I. (eds.). *Leading Beyond the Walls: How High-*

Performing Organizations Collaborate for Shared Success. San Francisco: Jossey-Bass, 1999, p. 156.

5. Bernard of Clairvaux. "On Consideration." In H. Fleiss, ed., *Essential Monastic Wisdom: Writings on the Contemplative Life.* San Francisco: Harper San Francisco, 1999.

6. Geneen, H., and Moscow, A. *Managing.* New York: Doubleday, 1984, p. 136.

7. Spears, L. C. "Tracing the Growing Impact of Servant-Leadership." In L. C. Spears, ed., *Insights on Leadership: Service, Stewardship, Spirit, and Servant-Leadership.* (5th ed.) New York: Wiley, 1998, p. 3.

8. Gardner, J. W. *On Leadership.* (9th paperback ed.) New York: Free Press, 1990, pp. 18 and 21.

9. Matusak, L. R. Finding Your Voice: Learning to Lead . . . Anywhere You Want to Make a Difference. (3rd ed.) San Francisco: Jossey-Bass, 1997, p. 149.

10. Wheatley, M. J. *Leadership and the New Science: Discovering Order in a Chaotic World.* (2nd ed.) San Francisco: Berrett-Koehler, 1999, p. 25.

11. Wheatley, 1999, p. 62.

12. Vaill, P. B. *Spirited Leading and Learning: Process Wisdom for a New Age.* San Francisco: Jossey-Bass, 1998, p. 110.

13. Vaill, 1998, p. 233.

14. O'Toole, J. *Leadership from A to Z: A Guide for the Appropriately Ambitious.* San Francisco: Jossey-Bass, 1999, pp. 135–136.

15. O'Toole, 1999, p. 226.

16. Beecher, H. W. "Ulysses S. Grant." In P. Theroux, ed., *The Book of Eulogies: A Collection of*

Memorial Tributes, Poetry, Essays, and Letters of Condolence. (4th ed.) New York: Scribner, 1997, p. 58.

17. Drucker, P. F. *The Effective Executive.* (40th paperback ed.) New York: HarperCollins, 1985, p. 148.

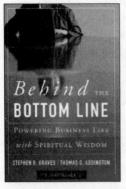

OTHER BOOKS OF INTEREST

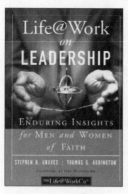

Life@Work on Leadership
Enduring Insights for Men and Women of Faith
Stephen R. Graves and
Thomas G. Addington
$19.95 Hardcover
ISBN: 0-7879-6420-4

"The worlds of leadership and faith were meant to be married. Never separated, never at odds, and never in competition. They were never intended to stand on opposite sides of the room, lonely and isolated, staring at each other."

—From the Foreword by Ken Blanchard

Using a Christian faith perspective, *Life@Work on Leadership* is a collection of selected readings from established leadership gurus that offers foundational writings on the integration of faith and work.

STEPHEN R. GRAVES and THOMAS G. ADDINGTON are the cofounders of Cornerstone Group, a consulting firm specializing in change management and strategy, and they are the cofounders of *Life@Work*, a journal that blends biblical wisdom with business excellence.

[Price subject to change]